FREE INDEED

Lessons from Jesus' Miracles

The Gospel of John

BY MICHAEL MACK

STANDARD PUBLISHING
Cincinnati, Ohio

TABLE of CONTENTS

All Scripture quotations, unless otherwise indicated, are taken from the HOLY BIBLE, NEW INTERNATIONAL VERSION®. NIV®. Copyright © 1973, 1978, 1984 by International Bible Society. Used by permission of Zondervan Publishing House. All rights reserved.

Cover design by
Steve Diggs & Friends

Inside design by
Liz Howe Design
Cover photo by
PhotoDisc

Edited and developed by
Jim Eichenberger

Contributing author
Mathew Sheep (Lesson 1)

©1999 by The Standard Publishing Company
All rights reserved.
Printed in the U.S.A.

Solid Foundation is an imprint from The Standard Publishing Company, Cincinnati, Ohio. A division of Standex International Corporation.

06 05 04 03 02 01 00 99
5 4 3 2 1

HOW TO USE THIS BOOK   3

Lesson 1
Jesus frees us from religious ritual.   4
John 2:1-11

Lesson 2
Jesus frees us from our self-imposed limitations.   14
John 4:43–5:18

Lesson 3
Jesus frees us from natural limitations.   24
John 6:1-59

Lesson 4
Jesus frees us from our blind spots.   34
John 9:1-41

Lesson 5
Jesus frees us from our fear of death.   44
John 11:1-57

Lesson 6
Jesus frees us from our past mistakes.   54
John 21:1-23

SOLID FOUNDATION BIBLE STUDIES

HOW TO USE THIS BOOK

Your adult Sunday school class or Bible study group probably contains people of different personalities from diverse backgrounds and with varying levels of biblical knowledge. *FREE INDEED—Lessons from Jesus' Miracles* is designed to equip you to teach biblical truths in ways that will reach every member of your class, regardless of his or her personality or background.

Each lesson contains valuable information to help you prepare your lesson. Pay special attention to the lesson title. It has been carefully crafted to communicate the main point of the study. This is the biblical truth that you want people to learn during the lesson and then apply during the days and weeks to come. Next, read the **Lesson Objectives.** They explain how the lesson will encourage people to discover and apply the main point of the study to their own lives. Finally, use the **Scripture Commentary** to deepen your own understanding of God's Word. The insights and biblical background within this section will prepare you to teach God's Word just as you would like—with excellence and with confidence.

Furthermore, the body of each lesson has been carefully constructed to take students where they are and then lead them into a discovery and personal application of the truths of God's Word. To accomplish this, each lesson body contains the following three sections:

In the Beginning. . . This opening activity introduces learners to the lesson topic and whets their appetites for the biblical content to follow. Use it to focus students' minds on the issue at hand and to open their hearts to receive God's truths.

The Word. . . This is the heart of the lesson, a time for meaningful study of God's Word. Best of all, studying the Bible doesn't have to be dull, as you will soon discover when you use the varied learning activities provided by this book.

The Word Became Flesh. . . Bible study profits little if it makes no difference in people's daily lives. So each lesson concludes with a time of personal application. Invite learners to apply what they've learned right away. You'll be excited at how much more they learn—and what a difference it makes in their lives.

One of those application activities for each lesson is "The Follow-Through Factor." This reproducible take-home devotional guide will allow your learners to more fully explore the relevance of the lesson throughout the following week.

Finally, each lesson offers a number of learning activities that you can match to the different learning styles of your class members. The people in your group do not all learn in the same way, so you need to provide various types of learning activities in each lesson. That's why each lesson in this book offers a number of learning activities for you to choose from. In fact, each section of every lesson provides two options so you can choose the best possible activity for your particular group. In short, you can custom-design a lesson for your group.

You have the tools, so why wait? Prepare lessons that are uniquely your own. Lead your group in an enjoyable and effective study of the Word of God.

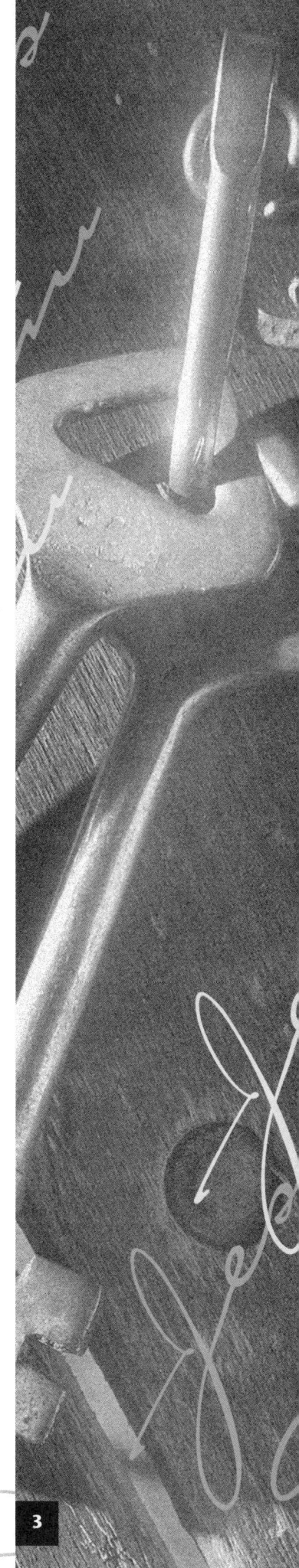

LESSON 1

Jesus frees us from religious ritual.

Lesson Objectives

In the course of this lesson, students will be able to

- *agree or disagree with the statement, "If people would only follow certain rules, the world would be a happier place."*
- *compare life in Jesus to religious ritual by using the symbols of water and wine.*
- *recall times in which we have settled for a "water" religion rather than the "wine" of Jesus.*

LESSON SCRIPTURE
John 2:1-11

SCRIPTURE COMMENTARY

America is one of the most religious, praying nations in the Western world. Yet U. S. rates of crime, teen pregnancy, abortion, and illegal drug use are higher than most in the world. What is wrong? Outward "religion" per se has proved powerless to stem the tide of inward, spiritual decay.

Jesus turned water into wine at a wedding feast at Cana in Galilee. John's inclusion of this miracle in his Gospel indicates its significance. It was "the first of his miraculous signs," it "revealed his glory," and it caused his newly-chosen disciples to "put their faith in him" (John 2:11). The theme of this sign seems to be, "Religion (water) is not enough. I come to bring new life (wine) from God."

Water, even in large supplies, can cleanse only from the outside. Wine, even in small amounts, works from the inside and "gladdens the heart of man" (Psalm 104:15). (Note the comparisons and contrasts of wine and the Holy Spirit in Acts 2:13-17 and Ephesians 5:18.) Under the Law (water, external religion) the best a person could hope for was to wash away surface guilt repeatedly. Jesus (wine, internal renewal) offered change from the inside — change that was abundant, free, and of the highest quality.

Religion (water) makes provision for cleansing people from the outside (2:1-7). Jesus used six water pots in this miracle to illustrate this truth. The water from the pots was used for ceremonial washing, constantly reminding the people of their need to be cleansed from their sins. To be ritually clean, those in the household would use water from those pots to wash both before and after meals. Utensils used for eating and cooking were also washed in this water.

In the preceding chapter, John proclaimed, "From the fullness of his grace we have all received one blessing after another. For the law was given through Moses; grace and truth came through Jesus Christ" (John 1:16, 17).

Law (water, external cleansing) and grace (wine, inward change) produce in people two very different mind-sets and motivations. Externally motivated law does not produce the greatest obedience to God or highest standards of

SOLID FOUNDATION BIBLE STUDIES

righteousness. The history of Israel in the Old Testament provides a multitude of examples.

One of the most explicit ways we can fall from grace is to return to a system of trusting in our own righteousness ("religion") to save us (Romans 10:3, 4; 11:5, 6; Galatians 5:4; Philippians 3:9). External religion ultimately frustrates and condemns all who seek to be justified by it because all are guilty of transgressing the very thing in which they trust to save them — perfect keeping of the law. (See Romans 3:20; Galatians 2:15, 16.)

Law-keeping results in destructive spiritual attitudes and habits. Predictably, a concentration on judging others — making sure people "get what they deserve" or "get what's coming to them" — is so easily produced by a mind-set based on law. This is logical, since a legal system of any kind depends upon *justice* (people getting what they deserve). In fact, a "system" itself can produce people who simply want to "beat the system." It cultivates no inner change, no rebirth, no new life generated from the inside out — but only self-reform by human effort, which to God is no more desirable than "filthy rags" (Isaiah 64:6; Romans 3:10-27).

Jesus (wine) makes provision for renewing people from the inside (2:8-11). Imagine what Jesus' disciples were thinking as Jesus ordered the servants to fill the water pots. Perhaps they recognized an Old Testament prophetic tone to Jesus' actions. Moses had confronted Pharaoh's sorcerers and the gods of Egypt (Exodus 7:8–8:19), and Elijah had challenged the prophets of Baal on Mount Carmel (1 Kings 18:16-40). Now, Jesus appeared to be setting up a similar contest between the Old and New Covenants.

To the same servants who filled the massive water pots he handed a small wineglass. "Now draw some out and take it to the master of the banquet," he ordered. When the wine touched the lips of the master of the banquet, the winner of this prophetic contest was obvious!

It is the "wine," the gift of God's grace in Christ Jesus, that God recognizes as our righteousness (2 Corinthians 5:21; Romans 4:4-11; 6:23; Titus 3:4-7). That's the good news! Grace produces an internal motivation based on faith expressing itself through love (Romans 13:8-10; Galatians 5:4-6), which is produced as a fruit of the Holy Spirit given at our baptism into Christ (Acts 2:38; Romans 5:5; Galatians 3:27). Grace produces a divine, internal change that transforms the mind and spirit to humbly desire God's will (Romans 12:1, 2), which comes from love for him (because he first loved us). Grace produces a mind-set that is more interested in seeing people receive the gift of God than their getting their just wages — what they deserve (Romans 6:23). Grace produces a desire to "go the extra mile" or "turn the other cheek" or become humbly obedient, even to the point of suffering (John 15:12, 13). (There is no law or threat of penalty that can make a person want to forsake self-will and self-interests; only love can do that.)

The Law and John the Baptist only pointed out sin, but Jesus would conquer it completely, so that we would "have life, and have it to the full" (John 10:10).

Further Insight

Some of Jesus' first disciples, including John the son of Zebedee were disciples of John the Baptist first (John 1:35-42). They probably had difficulty understanding the Baptist, who was usually spoke in very concrete terms, when he announced that while he baptized with water, Jesus would baptize with the Holy Spirit (John 1:26, 33). Note how many times in the early chapters of this Gospel that the themes of "water" vs. "spirit" are discussed (3:5; 4:10-14; 5:1-8; 6:16-21). Indeed, Jesus of Nazareth would do more than baptize repentant Jews. He would give his people new life from the water and the Spirit; he would cleanse those who had historically rejected the faith from the inside with living water; he would "stir" the healing waters within the afflicted; and literally march in victory over the surface of the waves!

IN THE BEGINNING...

Use one of the following activities to help learners agree or disagree with the statement, "If only people would follow certain rules, the world would be a happier place."

Would You Rather?
Time: 10-15 minutes

Divide the class into two groups. Give each group opposing statements to support. Allow each group one minute to list as many reasons as possible in support of its statement. Reasons may range from the thoughtful to the ridiculous.

The two statements are: **1. The world would be a better place if there were a strictly-enforced, written set of rules every one must follow; 2. The world would be a better place if there were no rules to live by.**

At the end of one minute, point to group one and ask for a reason in support of its statement. Quickly point to group two for a reason supporting the opposite view. Without time to comment, turn back to group one for another reason. Continue this rapid-fire approach until lists of both groups are exhausted.

Ask the "rules" group, **"What do you sacrifice to live by a strict set of rules?"** Lead them into concluding that personal freedom, creative thought, and individuality suffer when there is a strict rule of law. Then ask the "no rules" group, **"What do you sacrifice to live by no rules?"** Help them to articulate that security, order, and unity are sacrificed when law is abandoned.

Lead into Bible study with words similar to these: **"We seem to understand that there is a weakness in both totalitarianism (strict rule of law) and anarchy (absence of law). But is there another way?**

"During these next weeks we will look at the miracles of Jesus from the Gospel of John. John structured his Gospel around some specific miracles of Jesus. Each miracle illustrates the power Jesus has to solve life's biggest dilemmas. Today, let's look at a miracle that answers our question of the day. 'Is there a way we can live a life of both freedom and order?'"

Monarch for Minutes
Time: 15 minutes

Have the class choose someone creative to be the short-reigning (about 15 minutes) monarch of Waterville. The monarch has the privilege of enforcing only five rules (laws) that the class will try to obey for ten minutes while carrying out a series of tasks the monarch will assign verbally. Before beginning the tasks, make sure the monarch explains the laws to all of his subjects. (Take no more than five minutes for this.) He will read each one only twice.

THE FIVE LAWS
- **At no time will any of the monarch's subjects laugh or count out loud.**
- **Whenever one subject speaks to another subject, the spoken-to subject shall acknowledge by nodding his head twice.**

Materials Needed
- *sheets of paper and scissors for each person*

SOLID FOUNDATION BIBLE STUDIES

- **Whenever one subject nods his head twice to another subject, the nodded-to subject shall blink his or her eyes three times back at the nodder in acknowledgment.**
- **When any subject is talking, every other subject must place his or her right index finger on the tip of his or her own nose.**
- **When the monarch speaks, the subject who spoke most recently before the monarch spoke must bow to the monarch.**

At the instruction of the monarch, the rest of the class carries out the following tasks. The monarch keeps repeating these tasks until ten minutes have passed. The monarch of Waterville is responsible to stop the whole process and banish any offender of any of the above five laws from the room. The monarch will be alert to apprehend any and all subjects who are transgressors of these laws during the carrying out of the following tasks.

THE THREE TASKS
- **Rearrange the chairs in the room into a circle (or a square, or rows).**
- **Have the subjects hold hands and move clockwise in a circle.**
- **Provide sheets of paper and scissors to each subject. Have each subject cut out a different letter using his paper so that, when all of the letters are put together, they spell "Waterville." Have the subjects demonstrate.**

The object of this exercise is to create an environment ruled by strict law. "Depose" your monarch and debrief the activity with these questions. **"What do we sacrifice to live by a strict set of rules?"** Lead them into concluding that personal freedom, creative thought, and individuality suffer when there is a strict rule of law. Then ask, **"What do we sacrifice to live by no rules?"** Help them to articulate that security, order, and unity are sacrificed when law is abandoned.

Lead into Bible study with words from the end of the preceding activity.

THE WORD . . .

Use one of the following activities to help students compare life in Jesus to religious ritual by using the symbols of water and wine.

Interactive Lecture

Time: 20-30 minutes

Prepare an interactive lecture based on the **Scripture Commentary** for this lesson. Before class, write the Scripture passages you will have read on index cards. Hand each card to a volunteer and ask him or her to read the selected passage at the appropriate time.

Begin with the introductory comments in the first four paragraphs. Include students in this time by having them read the Bible passages as you come to them, especially Acts 2:13-18 and Ephesians 5:18. Before moving on, be sure the class understands the symbolic nature of this miracle.

Materials Needed

↪ index cards, each with a Scripture passage to be read; a picture of water pots

Ask the designated volunteer to read John 2:1-7. Then speak briefly about the next section, **"Religion (water) makes provision for cleansing people from the outside."** Find a Bible encyclopedia or other reference to show students a picture of such a water pot.

Under the statement, "We notice three things about externally motivated law," discuss each of the three points separately, and ask the following questions:

Under point one, ask, **"Can you recall a time in the Old Testament when Israel was not obedient to God?"** Using that example, follow up by asking, **"Since the people had the law from God, why were they still disobedient to him?"** *(The law had not brought about an inward change — a change of heart.)*

Under point two, ask, **"What is a way in which people tend to try to trust in their own righteousness (or religion) to save them?"** *(Examples include going to church, tithing, serving.)*

Under point three, ask, **"What are some examples of how a law and justice system can bring about destructive spiritual attitudes?"** Then ask, **"If a person were steeped in a legalistic mind-set that produced a judgmental attitude, what do you think would be the best way to help him or her out?"**

Transition the responses to this question into the next section, **"Jesus (wine) makes provision for renewing people from the inside."** Ask the designated volunteer to read John 2:8-11. During your brief lecture in this section, explain that wine has often been used for medicinal purposes (Luke 10:34; 1 Timothy 5:23). Some doctors have claimed that it has a cleansing effect on the body. While the Bible commands not to get drunk on wine, it is used here as a symbol of internal renewal that Jesus brings by his grace.

The **Scripture Commentary** suggests that grace produces four things. You may want to outline these four things on the chalkboard as you discuss them. Use the following questions to lead a brief discussion.

- **How does the Holy Spirit produce this internal motivation on a day-to-day basis?** *(Galatians 5:25 says, "Since we live by the Spirit, let us keep in step with the Spirit.")*
- **How can we keep in step with the Spirit?** *(Suggest a daily time spent with God through study of his Word and prayer.)*
- **How do we come to know God's will?** *(If you have not already, read Romans 12:1, 2. God will reveal his will to us as we stop being conformed to the ways of the world and, instead, allow the Spirit to transform our minds. Again, this can happen only as we spend time regularly with God.)*
- **Let's be honest with ourselves. Are you really more interested in people receiving the gift of God than getting their just wages? If so, what should each of us do about it?**
- **Someone described evangelism as one beggar sharing bread with another beggar. What does that mean to you?**

SOLID FOUNDATION BIBLE STUDIES

End this discussion by saying, **"Receiving God's grace through Jesus brings about internal changes in the life of a Christian — like the way wine can cleanse the inside of a sick body. Some of this cleansing happens when we first become Christians as we are baptized into Christ and receive his Spirit. But it is a continual process as well. Every day as we walk with the Spirit, we should be changed by his conviction. God is not done with any of us yet."**

Water and Wine Group Study

Time: 20-25 minutes

Ask a volunteer to read John 2:1-11. Then say, **"This was Jesus' first miracle. Today we will concentrate on the symbolism contained in this miracle."** Use selected portions of the **Scripture Commentary** to explain the symbolic nature of the water (religion) and the wine (Jesus). Before moving on, be sure the class understands the symbolism involved in this miracle Jesus performed.

Before class, cut the "Water and Wine" study sheet into the four sections. (If you anticipate having more than four groups, make several copies of the study sheet first so that more than one group can study a particular section.) Divide the class into groups of no more than eight people each and distribute a portion of the study sheet to each group. Before beginning their assignments, each group should select a spokesperson, who will summarize what the group has learned for the rest of the class. Instruct the groups to read their assigned passages, read the brief commentary statement, and answer the questions as a group.

After about ten minutes of study, tell the groups they have two minutes remaining. After twelve minutes, ask them to stop and turn their attention again to you. Ask the spokesperson of each group to summarize the group's findings. As they summarize what they learned, supplement their responses with these comments, as needed.

Materials Needed

- worksheet from page 11, cut into quarters for groups

Group 1

Through Moses and Aaron, God miraculously turned the water into blood, symbolizing destruction and death. Jesus turned water into wine, symbolizing new life from within that he would bring through his death on the cross.

Group 2

Water itself only cleansed the outside of a person. The baptism Jesus brought transformed a person from the inside through the gift of the Holy Spirit.

Group 3

Both the rebirth (water) and the gift of the Holy Spirit (Spirit) are necessary for a person to enter the kingdom of God. That does not mean the water of baptism itself has any power. But the act of baptism as Jesus modeled and commanded is an integral part of a person's rebirth into new life and receiving of the Holy Spirit.

Group 4

In both cases — being drunk on wine and being filled with the Holy Spirit—a person

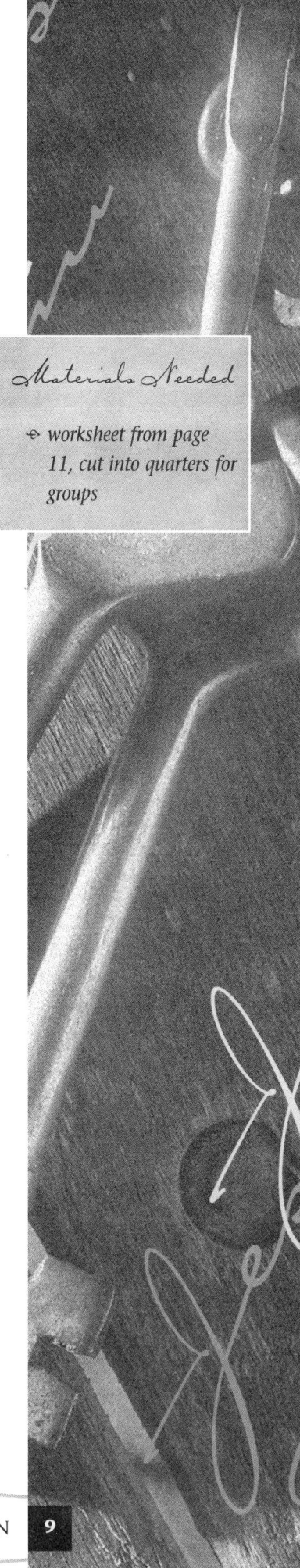

is "filled" with something that works from the inside out. The positive properties of wine—its medicinal properties—cleanses a person inside. The negative properties of wine make a person do things he would not ordinarily do if he were not drunk. The Holy Spirit can have the same effects on a person.

End this discussion with the words from the end of the preceding activity.

THE WORD BECAME FLESH . . .

Use one of the following activities to help students recall times in which they have settled for a "water" religion rather than the "wine" of Jesus.

Water People and Wine People

Time: 12-15 minutes

Divide the class into two groups of no more than ten people each. (In larger classes, divide up into as many groups as necessary, making sure you have an even number of groups.) Distribute a copy the worksheet to each person in the class. Have one group discuss how "water" people would observe the following activities — or the significance such activities might have to them. Have them write their conclusions on the chart. Have the other group discuss the same for "wine" people and write their conclusions on the chart. Share the findings and contrast them.

In addition or in place of the above activity, close by saying, **"Bill Hybels, senior pastor at Willow Creek Community Church in South Barrington, Illinois, says he uses an opening question with non-Christians to pique their curiosity: 'If you'd ever like to know the difference between religion and Christianity, let me know. I'd be happy to talk to you about it.' Many people respond by saying, 'I thought Christianity was a religion!' If you had this opportunity to talk to a non-Christian acquaintance about your faith, based on today's study, how would you respond to their comment about religion and Christianity?"** Allow several people to answer. Then say, **"Hybels suggests using a 'Do versus Done' approach. Religion is spelled D-O. We must *do* good things to be right with God. Christianity is spelled D-O-N-E. Everything we need to have a relationship with God has been done by Jesus when he died on the cross for us."**

The Follow-through Factor

Time: 5 minutes

This section appears in every lesson in this series. This weekly devotion plan helps class members apply the Bible study throughout the coming week. You may use it immediately after the Bible study or in conjunction with the preceding activity.

Give each person a copy of the handout. Take time to briefly read through it, but do not discuss any of the questions at this time.

Close the session in prayer.

Materials Needed

↦ copies of the work sheet from page 12

Materials Needed

↦ one copy of "The Follow-Through Factor" handout from page 13 for each person

WATER & WINE BIBLE STUDY

Group 1

Water Study

Read Exodus 7:14-21.

This is the first miracle that Moses performed.

What would happen to the life contained in the river after it was turned to blood? What does the blood in this Old Testament miracle symbolize? How does this compare to the symbolism of wine in Jesus' first miracle?

Wine Study

Read Psalm 4:7.

This Psalm was written by King David as he faced uncertain circumstances.

How is the contrast between inward joy and outward happiness described here? How are grain and new wine compared to being filled with God's Spirit?

Group 2

Water Study

Read John 1:29-34.

John baptized in water for repentance in preparation for the coming of Jesus.

How was Jesus' baptism different from John's? (See Acts 19:1-5.) What did the water of John's baptism do to the *inside* of a person?

Wine Study

Read Mark 2:22.

As new wine fermented, it expanded. An old wineskin could burst from the pressure. The new wine in this parable is Jesus himself and his new approaches to "doing religion."

How was the religion of the Pharisees like old wineskins? How is Jesus like new wine?

Group 3

Water Study

Read John 3:3-6.

Jesus is speaking to Nicodemus, one of the Pharisees. By "water and Spirit," he may be contrasting the physical birth (water) and the spiritual birth (Spirit) or he may be describing the repentance and rebirth of a person in water baptism and the receiving of the Holy Spirit.

How is Jesus' explanation different from Nicodemus's understanding of religion? Does the water or the Spirit cleanse a person from within?

Wine Study

Read Acts 2:13-18.

When the Holy Spirit came upon the disciples on the Day of Pentecost, they began to speak in other tongues, which the people could understand in their own native languages. This amazed the onlookers.

How are wine and the Holy Spirit compared here? How is being drunk on wine and being filled with the Spirit similar? Different?

Group 4

Water Study

Read John 4:7-15.

Jesus stopped at a well in Samaria to speak with a woman there. He used the symbolism of water from the well to talk with her about "living water," that is, himself. Later in this narrative, Jesus taught the woman about the difference between religion (vv. 21, 22) and true worship (vv. 23, 24).

What is the difference between the well water and "living water"? What can the well water do for this woman in the long run? What does this "living water" do for a person?

Wine Study

Read Ephesians 5:18.

Paul warns the Ephesian church about falling back into their old sinful habits, including drunkenness. The new life of a Christian should be marked by living by the Spirit rather than by the world's standards.

What kind of "high" does getting drunk on wine produce? How does that compare to being filled with the Holy Spirit?

WATER PEOPLE AND WINE PEOPLE

ACTIVITY	"WATER" PEOPLE	"WINE" PEOPLE
Singing		
Bible Study		
Giving		
Prayer		
Listening to a Sermon		
The Lord's Supper		
Helping a Neighbor		
Baptism		
Leisure Time & Recreation		
Witnessing		
Occupation		
Family Life		

SOLID FOUNDATION BIBLE STUDIES

THE FOLLOW-THROUGH FACTOR
Jesus frees us from religious ritual

Consider the implications of your last Bible study through this next week.

Monday
Read John 2:1-7 and 2 Timothy 3:5.

If you attended a worship service yesterday, write below any times that you simply went through the motions (a form of godliness) without inward involvement and worship (the power of godliness). Be honest. You don't have to show this to anyone but God.

Tuesday
Read John 2:8-11 and Matthew 5:3-6.

What is the "wine" in each Beatitude (Matthew 5:3-6)? In other words, how does each character trait have power to transform your life into a better follower of Jesus Christ?

Wednesday
Read John 2:1-11 and Matthew 5:7-10.

Again, what is the "wine" in each of these Beatitudes (Matthew 5:7-10)? How does each character trait have power to transform your life as a better follower of Jesus Christ?

Thursday
Read Romans 7:4-6.

What does Paul mean by the "new way of the Spirit" versus the "old way of the written code"? List one thing you have done today (or will do) that reflects your life in the "new way of the Spirit."

Friday
Read Galatians 5:1-6.

The weekend is at hand. List two leisure or family activities you intend to accomplish or two projects around the house on which you intend to work. These will all demand that choices be made consistant with these verses.

Saturday
Read Romans 12:1, 2.

How will your experience of worship tomorrow be changed by what you have studied this week? List at least one way in which you anticipate more than just being in attendance tomorrow, but being "transformed" by your worship of God.

LESSON 1 13

LESSON 2

Jesus frees us from our self-imposed limitations.

Lesson Objectives

In the course of this lesson, students will be able to
- list attitudes that keep people from doing their best.
- outline the three negative attitudes which Jesus confronted in the healings John describes.
- give examples of how the power of Christ can help us overcome those very attitudes.

LESSON SCRIPTURE
John 4:43–5:18

SCRIPTURE COMMENTARY

We often limit what God can do by planning too small, dreaming too small, building too small, giving too small, expecting too small. We build walls in the church that hold back God's blessings upon us. In two miracles in John 4 and 5, we see how Jesus can free us from these kinds of self-imposed and self-defeating limitations.

Jesus frees us from a "seeing is believing" mentality (4:43-54). A royal official traveled to Cana from Capernaum and asked Jesus to heal his son. This official was used to giving a command and having it obeyed. Surely he hoped for Jesus to go home with him and bring about a miraculous healing.

Most of us would have been shocked by Jesus' first reply: "Unless you people see miraculous signs and wonders, you will never believe." But the faith of this man was undaunted, and he renewed his request. You or I may have been further disappointed with Jesus' second reply: "You may go. Your son will live." But this official showed his faith again as he obeyed Jesus and headed for home.

The official's faith is further confirmed when he returned home, and on seeing his recovered son, he led his entire family to faith in Christ. We can only wonder if he and his family, and perhaps others they touched, were among the early believers in Capernaum when the church was birthed there years later.

Jesus frees us from a "poor me" mentality (5:1-9a). For thirty-eight years this man had been an invalid. He had no one to help him. No friends. No hope. No future. No purpose in life. Into this desperate situation steps Jesus.

"Do you want to get well?" What a question! The answer would seem obvious: Yes! But is that always true? For some people, a physical condition becomes such a way of life that their identity is wrapped up in the illness. Getting well means changing the way they look at themselves and the way others look at them. It means changing their lifestyle: getting a job, not relying on others or the government for assistance. The man would have to stand on his own two feet. People would no longer take pity on him. He would have to stop feeling sorry for himself.

Jesus stirred the man's faith. He dispelled any despondency that may have lingered in his heart. And he challenged the man: "Do you *really* want to get well? Are you sure? Are you ready to face changes in your life?" The man responded with a "poor me" mentality rather than faith: "I have no one to help me."

Another source of the "poor me" mentality takes the form of superstitious belief. Forces outside oneself are assumed to be at work, rendering the individual powerless. The lame man apparently believed that the first person into the pool after it had been "stirred" would be healed. This pool was probably fed by an underground spring, which would intermittently send a rush of bubbling water into the pool. Sick people evidently believed there was therapeutic value in the bubbling water, and that healing was granted only to the first one in the pool. Those in the right place at the wrong time could count themselves as helpless victims of powers beyond their control.

Note that Jesus did not directly attack the superstitious belief of the man and others. He simply showed them a *true* miracle directly from God. He sealed this act by ordering the man to pick up his own mat and walk through the busy city streets on the Sabbath. The attention it was sure to cause voiced a testimony to the people and the man himself: "You don't need to pity me anymore. I'm healed!"

Jesus frees us from an "it's against the rules" mentality (5:9b-18). The Pharisees witnessed both the miracle and the broken law. They chose to disregard the healed man and concentrate on a broken rule.

Sometimes people miss seeing the way God is moving because they are caught up in religious traditions. They limit God's power in their own lives and in his church because they have built walls around what they perceive the church to be. Jesus helps to free us from this mentality in his response to the Pharisees.

The Sabbath laws are found in Exodus 20:10, 11; 23:12; 31:12-17; Jeremiah 17:21. The Pharisees had added many impractical regulations to the original law. Mercy for this poor man was beside the point to them. A law had been broken!

Of course, this matter of law versus grace was a constant area of struggle between the Pharisees and Jesus. The Pharisees made laws to make sure people rested on the Sabbath. Jesus taught that it is only through love and mercy and doing the work of God seven days a week that one can find true rest and peace. Jesus told the Pharisees that his Father was always at work, as was Jesus himself. If God ever stopped "working for the good," the universe would collapse! The work of creation may have stopped after the sixth day, but the work of compassion continues, even to this day. The Sabbath was designated as a day of rest, not necessarily a day to cease from doing good—as the Jews self-imposed rules regulated against.

How can the church today "stop playing church and start being the church"? We see the answers in these miracles. Jesus is willing to act in ways unbounded by our senses or expectations. He can heal the brokenness of those who are tempted to be content with the minor comforts of self-pity. And our Savior displays goodness and justice and mercy that transcend cold rules and regulations. He sets his people free from the prisons they construct for themselves!

It's Greek to Me

*Here is another water vs. spirit illustration from the one-time disciple of John the Baptist. (See the **Scripture Commentary** from lesson one.)*

The word translated as "stirred" (5:7) is "tarasso." Other Greek words are used when speaking of something being "stirred up" from the outside. This particular word is usually translated "troubled," denoting being stirred up from internal conflict (John 12:27; 13:21; 14:1, 27). Jesus is compared to this spring at Bethesda. He is not just a water savior that cleanses from the outside, but he agitates from within, causing real and lasting change.

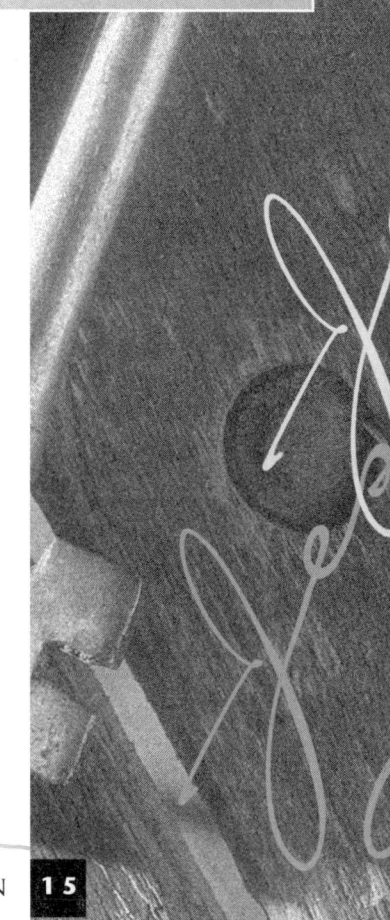

IN THE BEGINNING...

Use one of the following activities to help learners list attitudes that keep people from doing their best.

Focus on the Issue

Time: 10-15 minutes

Before class begins, place a copy of "Focusing In" at each seat. As students enter, ask them to take a few moments to work on the sheet.

As time draws near for class to begin, draw students' attention to the chalkboard where you've written a heading, "Attitudes That Keep People From Doing Their Best." Ask students to share some of the words or phrases that their lists have in common. Write these on the board or transparency as students call them out.

Some sample responses include, *I'm too young; I'm too old; I'm too poor; I'll never be able to make a difference anyway; everyone is against me; I don't have enough education; I can never get organized; there's nothing I really care that much about; I have a dysfunctional family; I have no support from my spouse; I never have enough hours in my day.*

Once you have a good representation from the class, ask students to look at this list and decide which ones are real limitations (such as physical ailments) and which are imaginary or mere excuses. Underline the real limitations and circle those that are imaginary or excuses. (Some, of course, will fall into other categories, such as "It all depends.") As the teacher, act as a translator (listening to and accepting the students' way of thinking) rather than as a transmitter (assuming that your way of thinking—or anyone else's—is the only way or the best way).

Next, ask students to look just at the circled responses (those that are imaginary or mere excuses). Ask them to try to connect several of the words or phrases that might belong in one category. Direct their attention to the bottom of the handout. Ask students to write a statement that summarizes these words or phrases. For instance, a statement might read, *Poor time management keeps many people from doing their best.* (Only use this example if students seem to struggle with understanding the assignment.)

Transition into the Bible study by saying, **"As we have seen, there are many reasons people do not achieve. Sometimes these reasons have legitimacy. Some limitations are there that do make success more difficult to achieve. Other times, however, our own attitudes hinder us and hold us back. So many times we sabotage our own best efforts.**

"In John 4 and 5, Jesus deals with three real or imagined self-imposed limitations. He frees people from a 'seeing is believing' mentality, a 'poor me' mentality, and an 'it's against the rules' mentality."

Materials Needed

- copies of the "Focusing In" handout from page 21; pens or pencils; chalkboard

SOLID FOUNDATION BIBLE STUDIES

Graffiti Walls

Time: 10-12 minutes

Before class, place one or two sheets of newsprint (or butcher paper) on the walls of the room. The heading on the top of the sheet should read,

Self-Imposed Limitations

I'm too _____ to be able to do my best.

Direct students as they enter the room to write in the space below the heading a word or short phrase that fits for them or for people in general. (Examples are *old, young, busy, short, slow*.) In addition to answering with words alone they may illustrate responses with simple line drawings.

Promote discussion about this subject as students settle in. Help them put the responses into categories. Do some responses deal with physical disabilities? Do some deal with time constraints? Do some seem to be excuses rather than valid reasons? Then, once everyone is seated and ready for class to begin, take a vote as to the top five self-imposed limitations that most people face today.

Ask, **"Why do you think we impose limitations on what we can do?"** After a few responses, ask, **"What other limitations do we impose — on others, on the church, even on God, for instance?"**

Transition into the Bible study by saying, **"As we have seen, there are many reasons why people do not achieve. Sometimes these reasons have legitimacy. Some limitations are there that do make success more difficult to achieve. Other times, however, our own attitudes hinder us and hold us back. So many times we sabotage our own best efforts.**

"In John 4 and 5, Jesus deals with three real or imagined self-imposed limitations. He frees people from a 'seeing is believing' mentality, a 'poor me' mentality, and an 'it's against the rules' mentality."

Materials Needed

↳ newsprint, markers

THE WORD . . .

Use one of the following activities to help students outline the three negative attitudes which Jesus confronted in the healings John describes.

No Way, No How, No Can Do

Time: 20-25 minutes

Divide the class into groups of three to five students each. Distribute a copy of the handout to each group. Instruct groups to follow the instructions at the top of the page by circling words or phrases that indicate negative attitudes of the people with whom Jesus came in contact. Give them a few minutes to do this. When all have finished, ask them to list some of the phrases they circled. If any of the following phrases are *not* listed, be sure to mention them before moving on to the next part of this activity: *"Unless you see . . . you will never believe"*; *"I have no*

Materials Needed

↳ copies of the "No Way, No How, No Can Do" handout from page 22; pens or pencils

one to help me . . . someone else goes down ahead of me"; "the law forbids you to carry your mat."

Next, have groups give their answers to the three questions on the bottom of the sheet. Below are some suggested responses.

1. **What negative attitude did the people have about Jesus and his miracles?** *They did not believe unless they saw evidence. They did not accept Jesus' work by faith alone. They had to be convinced of Jesus' power over and over again. They had a "seeing is believing" mentality that hindered them.*

2. **What negative attitude did the lame man have about his circumstances?** *The lame man focused on his conditions rather than the power of God. He used his circumstances as an excuse for giving up hope. His "poor me" mentality stood in the way of experiencing what Jesus wanted for him.*

3. **What negative attitude did the Jews have about the lame man being healed by Jesus?** *They witnessed a remarkable miracle, but refused to acknowledge it. Rather than rejoice at the fact that the lame man was freed from his disability, they chose to chastise him for breaking their religious regulations. Their "it's against the rules" mentality made them cold, unfeeling, and joyless.*

After all groups have reported, discuss each of the three negative mentalities—a "seeing is believing" mentality, a "poor me" mentality, and an "it's against the rules" mentality. Refer to the **Scripture Commentary** as necessary to explain these negative attitudes.

Close this section of the lesson with words similar to these: **"The miracles described in today's text have a powerful message! John describes people who were tempted to settle for less that God wanted to give them. By taking a "seeing is believing," "poor me," or "it's against the rules" approach to God's grace they created self-imposed limitations. Do we make similar mistakes? Let's consider that question more fully."**

Teaching to Learn

Time: 25-30 minutes

Divide the class into three groups. If you teach a class larger than 24 people, you may have more groups. More than one group may study a particular section.

Give each group a passage to study:

Group 1 — John 4:43-54

Group 2 — John 5:1-9a

Group 3 — John 5:9b-18

Give these instructions to the groups: **"After reading your passage, determine as a group what self-imposed limitations or negative attitudes are displayed by the people Jesus came in contact with. You will have ten minutes for discussion. Discuss these questions: 'Why would this person**

Materials Needed

- *chalkboard, copies of* **Scripture Commentary** *(one for each group)*

SOLID FOUNDATION BIBLE STUDIES

or people have the attitude they have? How do their self-imposed limitations affect their faith?'" You may want to write these questions on a chalkboard for all the groups to see:

- **What self-imposed limitations or negative attitudes are displayed by the people Jesus came in contact with?**
- **Why would this person or people have the attitude they have?**
- **How do their self-imposed limitations affect their faith?**

Distribute copies of the **Scripture Commentary** to each group. Have one person from the group read the section that pertains to their group. Ask them to discuss how the commentary compares with what they have already discussed. What insights does it add to their understanding?

Then direct students to find a creative way of teaching their part of the lesson to the rest of the class. They have only seven minutes to prepare and five to eight minutes for each group to teach. They may perform a skit, write a newspaper article describing the events, put on a newscast about the events, interview an eyewitness to the events, or draw a series of cartoon-type pictures to show how the events unfolded.

After seven minutes, have each group share its creative activity with the rest of the class. Comment upon each presentation as necessary to make sure the message is accurate and complete. Then close this section of the lesson with words similar to these: **"The miracles described in today's text have a powerful message! John describes people who were tempted to settle for less that God wanted to give them. By taking a "seeing is believing," "poor me," or "it's against the rules" approach to God's grace they created self-imposed limitations. Do we make similar mistakes? Let's consider that question more fully."**

THE WORD BECAME FLESH . . .

Use one of the following activities to help students give examples of how the power of Christ can help us overcome the negative attitudes Jesus confronted.

Responding to Jesus' Challenge

Time: 10 minutes

Distribute an index card or blank sheet of paper to each student. Ask students to write their responses to this question: **"If Jesus asked you, 'Do you want to get well?' what would he be asking about?"** They should consider physical, emotional, family, work, spiritual, and any other situations.

Ask volunteers to share their answers. You, as the teacher, may need to start by sharing a brief response.

As a person shares, you may ask, **"What attitudes or self-imposed limitations might keep you from getting well?"** Of course, use discretion as you

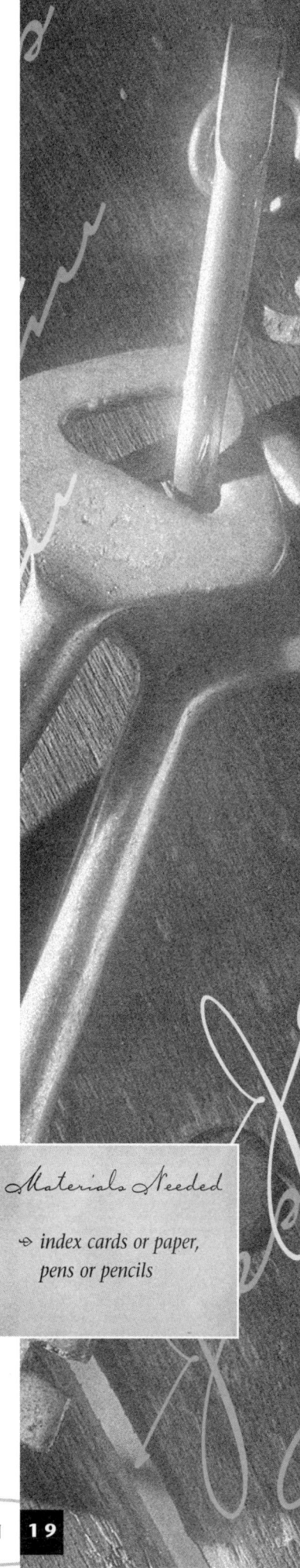

Materials Needed

↦ *index cards or paper, pens or pencils*

FREE INDEED

ask this question. You may wish to cultivate interaction among the class during this time, but be sure no one tries to "fix the problem" (that's Jesus' job) by offering unsolicited advice. This is a time to care for participants by listening and offering support and prayer. Be ready, in case someone shares a deep hurt, to lovingly comfort or encourage him or her. Take time to pray for the need right away, but be sure you don't pray simply as a way to avoid dealing with it or offering support.

Close the session with a quiet time of prayer. Say, **"Close your eyes and imagine that Jesus is right here beside you, just like he was beside the father whose son was dying or the man who had been paralyzed for thirty-eight years. He asks you, 'Do you want to get well?' and you respond to him. If you have faith that Jesus can bring healing to your situation, quietly ask him to do that now."**

After a few moments, close in prayer, asking God to give us the strength to live by faith and not by sight, to have the faith to allow Jesus to help us, and to live by grace and not by the law.

The Follow-through Factor

Time: 5 minutes

This section appears in every lesson in this series. This weekly devotion plan helps class members apply the Bible study throughout the coming week. You may use it immediately after the Bible study or in conjunction with the preceding activity.

Give each person a copy of the handout. Take time to briefly read through it, but do not discuss any of the questions at this time.

Close the session in prayer.

NOTES

Materials Needed

- one copy of "The Follow-Through Factor" handout from page 23 for each person

FOCUSING IN

A. In the spaces below, list six words or phrases that describe attitudes or outlooks on life that keep people from doing their best.

1. _____

2. _____

3. _____

4. _____

5. _____

6. _____

B. When finished with step A, find two or three others and compare your list with theirs. Look to see how many of your words or phrases are the same or similar to others'.

List below any words or phrases that your list has in common with others' lists.

1. _____

2. _____

3. _____

4. _____

Summary Statement of Self-Imposed Limitations:

NO WAY, NO HOW, NO CAN DO

Read through the Scripture passage below, circling words or phrases that indicate negative attitudes of the people with whom Jesus came in contact.

John 4:43–5:18

After the two days he left for Galilee. ⁴⁴(Now Jesus himself had pointed out that a prophet has no honor in his own country.) ⁴⁵When he arrived in Galilee, the Galileans welcomed him. They had seen all that he had done in Jerusalem at the Passover Feast, for they also had been there.

⁴⁶Once more he visited Cana in Galilee, where he had turned the water into wine. And there was a certain royal official whose son lay sick at Capernaum. ⁴⁷When this man heard that Jesus had arrived in Galilee from Judea, he went to him and begged him to come and heal his son, who was close to death.

⁴⁸"Unless you people see miraculous signs and wonders," Jesus told him, "you will never believe."

⁴⁹The royal official said, "Sir, come down before my child dies."

⁵⁰Jesus replied, "You may go. Your son will live."

The man took Jesus at his word and departed. ⁵¹While he was still on the way, his servants met him with the news that his boy was living. ⁵²When he inquired as to the time when his son got better, they said to him, "The fever left him yesterday at the seventh hour."

⁵³Then the father realized that this was the exact time at which Jesus had said to him, "Your son will live." So he and all his household believed.

⁵⁴This was the second miraculous sign that Jesus performed, having come from Judea to Galilee.

⁵:¹Some time later, Jesus went up to Jerusalem for a feast of the Jews. ²Now there is in Jerusalem near the Sheep Gate a pool, which in Aramaic is called Bethesda and which is surrounded by five covered colonnades. ³Here a great number of disabled people used to lie—the blind, the lame, the paralyzed. ⁵One who was there had been an invalid for thirty-eight years. ⁶When Jesus saw him lying there and learned that he had been in this condition for a long time, he asked him, "Do you want to get well?"

⁷"Sir," the invalid replied, "I have no one to help me into the pool when the water is stirred. While I am trying to get in, someone else goes down ahead of me."

⁸Then Jesus said to him, "Get up! Pick up your mat and walk." ⁹At once the man was cured; he picked up his mat and walked.

The day on which this took place was a Sabbath, ¹⁰and so the Jews said to the man who had been healed, "It is the Sabbath; the law forbids you to carry your mat."

¹¹But he replied, "The man who made me well said to me, 'Pick up your mat and walk.'"

¹²So they asked him, "Who is this fellow who told you to pick it up and walk?"

¹³The man who was healed had no idea who it was, for Jesus had slipped away into the crowd that was there.

¹⁴Later Jesus found him at the temple and said to him, "See, you are well again. Stop sinning or something worse may happen to you." ¹⁵The man went away and told the Jews that it was Jesus who had made him well.

¹⁶So, because Jesus was doing these things on the Sabbath, the Jews persecuted him. ¹⁷Jesus said to them, "My Father is always at his work to this very day, and I, too, am working." ¹⁸For this reason the Jews tried all the harder to kill him; not only was he breaking the Sabbath, but he was even calling God his own Father, making himself equal with God.

1. What negative attitude did the people have about Jesus and his miracles?

2. What negative attitude did the lame man have about his circumstances?

3. What negative attitude did the Jews have about the lame man being healed by Jesus?

SOLID FOUNDATION BIBLE STUDIES

THE FOLLOW-THROUGH FACTOR
Jesus frees us from our self-imposed limitations.

Consider the implications of your last Bible study through this next week.

Monday
Read John 4:43-45 and Revelation 3:19-21.
Write three ways you can make Jesus welcome in your life today. Take time to welcome him into the activities of your week. Invite him to be part of all your thoughts, decisions, actions, and attitudes.

Tuesday
Read John 4:46-50a; Mark 15:32; John 16:30; 20:25-29; and 2 Corinthians 5:7.
List at least one area in your life in which you have been living by sight.
Read Ephesians 3:14-21 and then pray it back to God in your own words.

Wednesday
Read John 4:50b-54 and John 4:39-42.
Whom in your sphere of influence can you bring to Jesus or tell about Jesus?
Pray for the person(s) on your list—that they may come to faith in Jesus and that you may have opportunities to share your faith with them.

Thursday
Read John 5:1-9a and Philippians 4:10-13.
Compare the paralyzed man's attitude with Paul's. Write at least three words that describe each one. Pray that you will have the faith of Paul who said, "I can do everything through him who gives me strength."

Friday
Read John 5:9b-13 and Nehemiah 13:15-22.
List several differences between what Jesus did on the Sabbath and what the merchants in Nehemiah's time were doing. Ask God to forgive you of attitudes that keep you from experiencing his working fully.

Saturday
Read John 5:14-18; Genesis 2:1-3; and Mark 2:23–3:6.
On the seventh day, from what work did God rest? Briefly state Jesus' view of the Sabbath and man's relationship to it. Ask God to show you the work he has for you to do today.

LESSON 2

LESSON 3
Jesus frees us from natural limitations.

Lesson Objectives

In the course of this lesson, students will be able to
- *complete the sentence, "If I could do the impossible, I would . . ."*
- *summarize the impossible feats Jesus performed in John 6.*
- *explain how serving the God of impossibilities can change our lives today.*

LESSON SCRIPTURE
John 6:1-59

SCRIPTURE COMMENTARY

In John 6, Jesus challenged the disciples' faith. What seemed impossible to them, he brought into the realm of the possible.

Jesus can nourish us when we have no food (6:1-15). Jesus crossed the sea to a solitary place, but the crowds caught up to him quickly. A problem arose. How would all these people get food to eat? Jesus pulled Philip into the situation. It was a teachable moment.

Philip responded to Jesus' question by figuring out the financial means necessary to take care of the need. Philip seems to be a problem solver, but he overlooked the best resource available—Jesus himself.

Andrew brought a small boy with a sack lunch. It wasn't much. Barley loaves were cheap bread, but they, along with a few small fish, would be sufficient to meet the hunger of the crowd.

Shortly after Dallas Theological Seminary was founded in 1924, it almost ceased to exist. President Lewis Chafer met with the faculty, praying fervently that God would provide. Dr. Harry Ironside prayed, "Lord, we know that the cattle on a thousand hills are Thine. Please sell some of them and send us the money."

Meanwhile, a Texas businessman stepped into the seminary business office, and said, "I have two carloads of cattle in Fort Worth, but could not make a deal go through. I feel compelled to give the money to the seminary. Here's the check!"

The secretary took the check and timidly knocked on Dr. Chafer's door. Chafer took the check, and it was for the exact amount of the debt. Turning to Dr. Ironside, Chafer said, "Harry, God sold the cattle!"

We live in a materialistic culture. We are taught that we could accomplish more if we had more money and more property. Jesus' miracle exposes that lie. *A savior who can nourish when there is no food can meet any material need we have.*

Jesus can direct us where there is no path (6:16-24). Jesus instructed his disciples to go ahead of him to the other side of the lake. Jesus went up on a mountainside to pray (Mark 6:45, 46). Jesus always prayed for God's will to be done in his own life, and he probably prayed for direction for his ministry.

SOLID FOUNDATION BIBLE STUDIES

While Jesus was still on land, the waters became rough. Though a storm like this was not unexpected to experienced fishermen, it still was scary. So Jesus responded to their need again. He walked across the lake to where they were.

People have asked just *how* Jesus performed this miracle. Did he make himself lighter than water, or did he change the water beneath his feet into ice so he could walk upon it? On that the Bible is silent. Yet an explanation of the miracle is far less important than its purpose.

The disciples were terrified when they saw Jesus walking across the water. According to Mark's gospel, the disciples thought Jesus was a ghost. That would be terrifying! Jesus responded to their fear. He did not belittle their real feelings. He told them to "Take courage!" (Mark 6:50). The wind died down as Jesus entered the boat with them, and immediately the boat reached the shore where they were heading.

We may not know where we are to go, especially as we endure difficult storms in our lives. But Jesus knows where to take us and is the only way to our eternal destination. We must allow him to climb into the boat lead the way. *A savior who can direct us where there is no path can guide us through the most tumultuous moments of life.*

Jesus can give us life in a world that knows only death (6:25-59). As he conversed with the crowds following these miracles, Jesus made it clear that he desires to overcome our greatest physical limitation. Not only will he meet our physical needs and our need for direction in times of trouble, but he will actually change the way we view our world.

The Jews could not think "outside the box" of the Pharisaical system of works righteousness. They responded to Jesus, "What must we *do* to do the works God requires?" Jesus challenges them to simply *believe* in the one God sent. So the Jews asked Jesus for a sign so that they might believe in him. Jesus had just multiplied a boy's lunch into enough food to feed more than 5,000 people!

The differences between Moses and Jesus illustrate the transition from the Old Covenant to the New Covenant (Hebrews 10:9-12). It was necessary for Moses' provision of manna in the desert to be repeated every day, until the Israelites entered the Promised Land. It did not last. Jesus' provision of the bread of life is provided once for all time. Those who eat of it will never go hungry (v. 35) and never die (vv. 50, 51).

Jewish law forbade the drinking or eating of any blood (Deuteronomy 12:23; Leviticus 17:10, 14). Yet Jesus used the words *flesh* and *blood* to represent everything needed to sustain life. If we do not accept Jesus' life-giving blood that he shed on the cross, we cannot have eternal life.

Because they clung to a view of the world in which death ruled, "many of his disciples turned back and no longer followed him" (John 6:66). What a tragedy! *A savior who can give us life in a world that knows only death can allow us to perceive our world and our need for a savior accurately.*

The very fact of our humanity gives us limitations. Yet Jesus allows us to overcome them. Through him our physical needs are met, our paths in life are directed, and our very perception of life is changed.

It's Greek to Me

The crowds followed Jesus to the other side of the lake because they wanted something from him. They wanted their bellies filled. In verse 26, the phrase "had your fill" is one word in the Greek, "echortasthete," which means, literally, "to give fodder to animals." These people were like animals— like wayward sheep — who just wanted to satisfy their physical desires. Jesus wanted to give them something that would last, but they kept searching for things that spoil (Matthew 6:19-21). He wanted to give everlasting life, but they kept searching for things that pass away. Things have not changed much over the years.

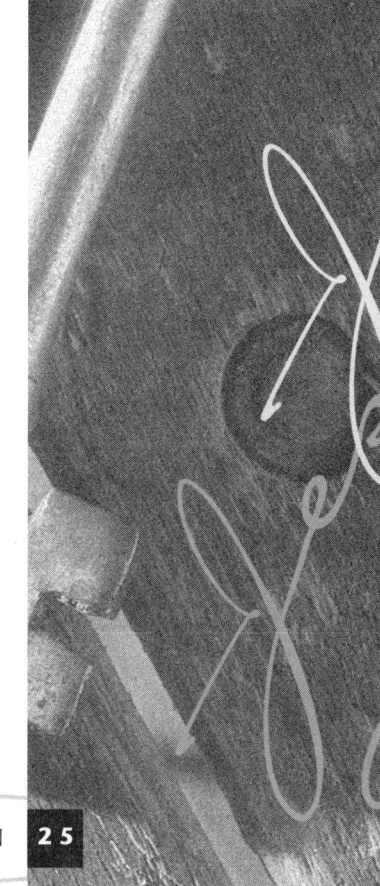

IN THE BEGINNING . . .

Use one of the following activities to help learners complete the sentence, "If I could do the impossible, I would . . ."

Outrageous Responses

Time: 15 minutes

Divide the class into groups of five or six people each. Number each group and have each group select a spokesperson. Begin the game by asking group 1, **"If *impossible* were not an option, what outrageous goal would you accomplish?"**

Play continues as group 2 answers the same question. Their answer, however, must begin with the last letter of the preceding groups response. In that manner continue play by posing the question to succeeding groups. Give each group thirty seconds to confer before asking for the spokesperson to respond.

A series of answers might be: *climb Mount Everes*t; *t*ake an ocean cruis*e*; *e*nter politic*s*; *s*talk wild game in Afric*a*; *a*ct in a television progra*m*; *m*ake millions in the stock market. When the chain is broken, skip to the next group and begin again. Play a few rounds, encouraging the most outrageous of answers.

Lead into the Bible study by saying, **"We obviously have some outrageous dreams! Of course, most people would say that these dreams are impossible."**

"In John 6, Jesus challenged the disciples' faith. What seemed impossible to them, he brought into the realm of the possible, and that changed their whole perspective on life.

"When our circumstances look impossible, where do we turn? Let's look at how Jesus' miracles demonstrated that he can overcome natural limitations."

Thinking Outside the Box

Time: 10-15 minutes

Before class, place a copy of the handout at each chair. As students enter, direct them to follow the instructions on the sheet. Allow them to work in groups if to find a solution if they would like.

After everyone has arrived, ask if anyone has accomplished any of the tasks. Each task was difficult because it required participants to think non-traditionally. In Task 1, traditional thinking would have had them cross out four of the sixteen letters in the box. They could solve the task by crossing out the words "four letters," thereby revealing the solution, *Paris*. What appears to be a single figure of intersecting lines in Task 2 can be seen as four separate arrows, designating the points on the compass, N, S, E, W. Interpreted in that way, the word, *sewn*, can be decoded. In Task 3, traditional thinking would look for a mathematical relationship between the numbers. The numerals were actually grouped by shape. Those in the first box were

---

Materials Needed

- one copy of the "Thinking Outside the Box" handout from page 31 for each person, pens or pencils

constructed of straight lines only, the second group with straight lines and curves, the third group with curves alone. Therefore the numerals should be grouped: *1, 4, 7; 2, 5;* and *0, 3, 6, 8, 9.*

Lead into the Bible study by saying, **"To solve these problems, you need to 'think outside the box.' They were impossible to solve without going outside the boundaries of traditional thinking. Many life situations seem impossible to us, too, but it may be that we just need to 'think outside the box' in those circumstances.**

"In John 6, Jesus challenged the disciples to view life outside of physical limitations. What seemed impossible to them, he brought into the realm of the possible, changing their whole perspective on life.

"When our circumstances look impossible, where do we turn? Let's look at how Jesus' miracles demonstrated that he can overcome natural limitations."

THE WORD . . .

Use one of the following activities to help students summarize the impossible feats Jesus performed in John 6.

Mission Impossible

Time: 25-30 minutes

Prepare a lecture using portions of the **Scripture Commentary** and including students in an activity for each section. Divide the class into three groups. These teams will take on "impossible" missions to solve three different problems.

For section one, "Jesus can nourish us when we have no food," ask a volunteer to read John 6:1-15. Begin by reading or paraphrasing the first two paragraphs of this section to the class. Then, give the groups this mission: **"Your mission, should you choose to accept it, is to imagine you are Philip and a few of the other disciples nearby. Jesus has given your team this problem to solve: How would you take care of the crowd's needs? Come up with as many creative solutions as you can in two minutes. Go."** (If you can secure a copy of the "Mission Impossible" theme song, play it in the background as students work.)

After two minutes, bring the class back together in discussion. Ask groups for a few of their better solutions. Then start with the third paragraph to create a mini-lecture about this material. Include the story about Dallas Theological Seminary, and then ask these questions:

- **How was the response of these men different from that of the disciples?**
- **How did the leaders of the seminary wisely use all of their available resources?**

Materials Needed

↝ *cassette or CD of "Mission Impossible" theme song (optional)*

FREE INDEED

Summarize this section with this thought, **"A savior who can nourish when there is no food can meet any material need we have."**

For section two, "Jesus can direct us where there is no path," ask a volunteer to read John 6:16-24. Begin your mini-lecture by reading or paraphrasing the first two paragraphs in this section. (It will be helpful for you to read the parallel passages, especially Mark 6:45-52 for this section beforehand.)

Say, **"Here is your second mission, should you choose to accept it: How did Jesus perform this miracle?"** Give students a few moments to think about this, and then, if no one responds, ask, **"Do you think he made himself lighter than water, or did he change the water beneath his feet into ice so he could walk upon it? Or something else? Discuss this in your groups for two minutes."**

Give groups two minutes to discuss this question. Have a few groups report their solutions back to the rest of the class. Then say something like, **"We tend to look at the physical conditions to explain things that have no explanation. What Jesus wants us to learn is that he is able 'to do immeasurably more than all we ask or imagine.' Instead of asking how, we need to respond with a childlike faith that he is able — he is sufficient for all our needs.**

"God is sovereign. That means he is in control over everything, including nature. He often allows things to happen for a variety of reasons we do not always understand, but he is in control. We may be unsure about the direction of our lives at times, especially as we go through difficult storms in our lives. But Jesus knows where to take us, and he has the way. *He* is the way, the truth, and the life. He is the only way to our eternal destination. We must allow him to climb into the boat with us and let him lead the way. A savior who can direct us where there is no path can guide us through the most tumultuous moments of life."

For section three, "Jesus can give us life in a world that knows only death," ask a volunteer to read John 6:25-59.

Then say, **"The Jews often missed the meaning of Jesus' teaching. Jesus was teaching something new. Throughout this passage, we see Jesus and the Pharisees looking at the world in two totally different ways."** Then give the groups this mission, **"List instances in this passage that show differences in how Jesus and the Pharisees viewed life."**

Give groups five minutes to study, and then ask them to report whatever explanations they discovered. Some possible responses are charted below.

Verses	Pharisees' view	Jesus' view
26, 27	Life is about meeting physical needs.	Life is about preparing for the world to come.
28, 29	We earn favor with God by our works.	We are granted favor with God by accepting Jesus.
30-40	Messiah will provide	Messiah will provide

SOLID FOUNDATION BIBLE STUDIES

	satisfaction of	eternal satisfaction.
	temporal needs.	
41-51	Jesus was a	He is the eternal
	human teacher.	Son of God.
52-59	We must remain	We can be pure only by
	pure by keeping	uniting ourselves
	religious ritual.	with Jesus.

Close the activity with words similar to these: **"The very fact of our humanity gives us limitations. Yet Jesus allows us to overcome them. Through him our physical needs are met, our paths in life are directed, and our very perception of life is changed. How does reliance upon an overcoming savior affect the way we live today?"**

Special Report

Time: 25-30 minutes

Before class, copy the resource sheet and cut it into three sections. Divide the class into three groups, and distribute one section of the resource sheet and a copy of the **Scripture Commentary** to each group. Ask the groups to imagine themselves as in-depth news reporters for GNN (Galilee News Network) covering the events in John 6. They will have fifteen minutes to prepare a hard-hitting news report, which they will give to the rest of the class. They may include brief interviews of witnesses, interviews of experts, straight narrative by a reporter, and any other news reporting they want to use.

As groups prepare, move among them to help them understand the passage about which they are reporting. Refer to the **Scripture Commentary** and the comments from the preceding activity to help you as necessary.

Each group will have about five minutes to report their news. After each report, comment as necessary to assure that content is summarized accurately and completely. Then close by saying: **"The very fact of our humanity gives us limitations. Yet Jesus allows us to overcome them. Through him our physical needs are met, our paths in life are directed, and our very perception of life is changed. How does reliance upon an overcoming savior affect the way we live today?"**

Materials Needed:

↪ prepared copy of the "Special Report" handout from page 32 and copies of the **Scripture Commentary**

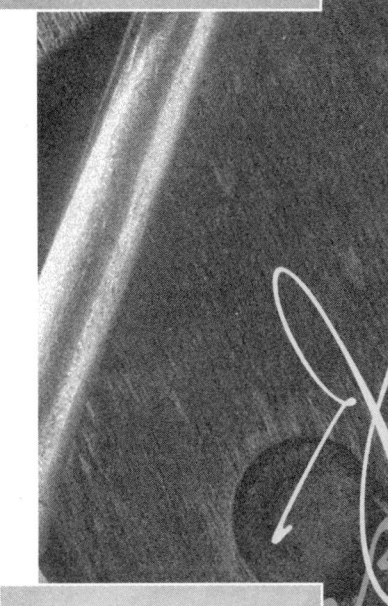

THE WORD BECAME FLESH . . .

Use one of the following activities to help students explain how serving the God of impossibilities can change our lives today.

All Things Are Possible Basket

Time: 5-10 minutes

Distribute a sheet of blank paper or index card, along with a pen or pencil

Materials Needed:

↪ sheets of paper or index cards, pens or pencils, basket or other suitable container

FREE INDEED

GOSPEL OF JOHN

to every participant. Ask students to take a moment and think about a situation in their lives that seems impossible and write it on the paper or card. Remind them of the areas in which Jesus demonstrated superiority in today's lesson: **meeting physical needs, giving direction in facing a problem, and changing how his disciples think about life.** Assure them that they do not have to show anyone else their response. In the front or middle of the room, place a basket with a sign on it with these words: **"What is impossible with men is possible with God"** (Luke 18:27), and ask students to bring their cards up and place them in the basket. Ask them to do this prayerfully, as if they were placing this in God's hands.

End class by having the class or several volunteers pray over the basket, telling God you are placing these things in his hands by faith. Praise God because he can make all things possible for those who believe.

The Follow-Through Factor

Time: 5 minutes

This section appears in every lesson in this series. This weekly devotion plan helps class members apply the Bible study throughout the coming week. You may use it immediately after the Bible study or in conjunction with the preceding activity.

Give each person a copy of the handout. Take time to briefly read through it, but do not discuss any of the questions at this time.

Close the session in prayer.

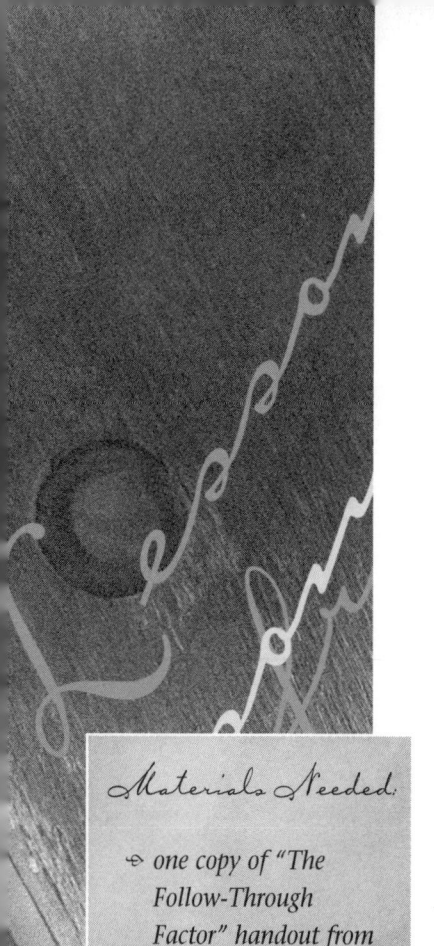

NOTES

Materials Needed:

- one copy of "The Follow-Through Factor" handout from page 33 for each person

SOLID FOUNDATION BIBLE STUDIES

SOLID FOUNDATION BIBLE STUDIES

THINKING OUTSIDE THE BOX

Before class begins, see if you can solve these three impossible tasks.

Task 1

Cross out four letters in the box below to spell the name of a famous city.

```
P F O A
U R R L
  I E T T
E S R S
```

Task 2

A simple word is encoded below. Break the code and reveal the word.

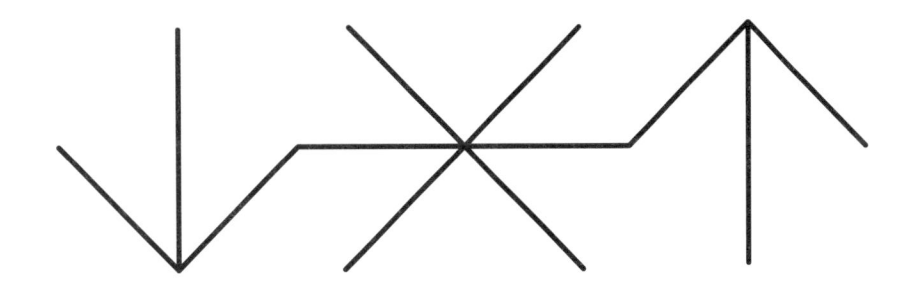

Task 3

The numerals 4-9 have been placed in three separate categories below. Place the numerals 0-3 in their proper categories.

| 4, 7 | 5 | 6, 8, 9 |

LESSON 3

SPECIAL REPORT

GROUP A

Read John 6:1-15.

Background Scriptures: Mark 6:1-44; Deuteronomy 18:15.

Questions to Consider: Why were these crowds following Jesus? Who was involved in making this miracle happen? What are some natural explanations for this so-called miracle? Where did the bread and fish come from? Why in the world would Andrew even consider bringing so little food to feed so many people? Will Jesus run for king next election?

GROUP B

Read John 6:16-24.

Background Scriptures: Mark 6:45-52; John 14:6

Questions to Consider: Where did Jesus go after he dismissed the crowds? Why? Where did his disciples go? Why? How did Jesus get to the other side of the lake? What are some natural explanations for him walking on the water? What did the disciples see from the boat? What did they *think* they saw? How did the disciples feel when they saw Jesus? What does the Nazareth Weather Service say about the weather that night? How did the disciples feel after Jesus got in the boat with them?

GROUP C

Read John 6:25-59.

Background Scriptures: Matthew 6:19-21; Hebrews 10:9-12; John 6:63; Deuteronomy 12:23; Leviticus 17:10, 14

Questions to Consider: Why did the crowds follow Jesus across the lake? How did they get there? What has caused the obvious communication problem between Jesus and the Jews? What are the Jews wanting Jesus to do? Why? What are the differences between these supposed miracles — the provision of manna in the desert and the feeding of the 5,000? What does it mean? How did the people feel and react to Jesus when he talked about eating flesh and drinking blood? What did Jesus really mean by his "flesh and blood" comments? What do the experts say? What do his followers say?

SOLID FOUNDATION BIBLE STUDIES

THE FOLLOW-THROUGH FACTOR
Jesus frees us from our natural limitations.

Consider the implications of your last Bible study through this next week.

Monday
Read John 6:1-3, 25, 26 and Mark 1:16-20.
   Why do you follow Jesus? (Be honest!)
If you have followed Jesus for selfish reasons, confess that to him now and repent of this attitude. Ask God to help you be a disciple who wants to do his will.

Tuesday
Read John 6:16-21; John 14:27; and Revelation 1:17, 18.
   In what specific area of your life do you need to hear Jesus say, "It is I; don't be afraid?"
Read Hebrews 13:6, and use it as your prayer today.

Wednesday
Read John 6:26-29 and Matthew 6:19-21.
   Where in your life are you working for "food that spoils" rather than "food that endures to eternal life"?
Meditate on Psalm 111, and put it into your own words as your thanksgiving prayer for all God provides.

Thursday
Read John 6:32-35 and John 4:7-15.
   For what physical things do you "hunger and thirst?"
Read Matthew 5:6; John 4:34. For what should we "hunger and thirst?"
Ask God to replace your hunger with his hunger for your life.

Friday
Read John 6:37-40, 44; John 12:32; 1 Corinthians 3:6-9; and 2 Corinthians 5:20.
   What is God's part in the salvation process? What is our part as his witnesses?

Saturday
Read John 10:53-58 and Matthew 26:26-29.
   Write a brief thank-you note to Jesus for giving his body and blood for you.

LESSON 3   33

LESSON 4

Jesus frees us from our blind spots.

Lesson Objectives

In the course of this lesson, students will be able to
- summarize the value of sight.
- compare and contrast ways that people reacted to the healing of the blind man.
- respond in specific ways to the vision God gives them as Christians.

LESSON SCRIPTURE
John 9:1-41

SCRIPTURE COMMENTARY

"There are none so blind as those that will not see." That is the truth conveyed in John 9, a story about a blind man who receives his physical sight and confounds the scholars of the day with straightforward belief and common sense reasoning.

The events of chapters six through eight set the stage for the healing of the blind man in chapter nine. The "Jews" could not see that Jesus was who he said he was—the Messiah, the Son of God, the Light—who came into the world to initiate a New Covenant. Giving sight to the blind was a prophecy of the Messiah (Isaiah 29:18; 35:5; 42:7). Giving sight to a person *born* blind, which was unheard of at that time, was further proof of Jesus' true identity and purpose.

The blind man accepted the gift of sight with his obedient faith (9:1-17, 25-38). The Pharisees taught that those who prospered did so because of their own purity, and the suffering of the afflicted was their own fault. Nevertheless the blind man in this chapter was blind since birth, blind before he had the opportunity to sin (v. 1)! The Pharisees attempted to answer this objection by teaching that one *could* sin before birth, either in the womb or as a pre-existing spirit. They also taught that a child could be born disabled as a result of his parent's sin.

The disciples echoed these teachings in their question to Jesus (vs. 2). Jesus did not let these hateful beliefs go unchallenged. The rich and whole are no more holy than the poor and afflicted. All have sinned. And he proceeded to demonstrate that all could be saved by faith in the One sent as light into the world (vv. 3-5).

Jesus had compassion on the man. The use of spittle and dirt in the healing may seem odd to us (v. 6). People of that time believed that saliva had healing power, and the saliva of an important person was particularly effective in healing the blind. The use of dirt in the miracle is interesting also. God created man from the dust of the ground. This man was born blind, so the use of dirt from the ground conjures up the idea of re-creation of the man's sight.

Note the interdependence of faith and obedience. The man was healed totally apart from his own power, yet his obedience confirmed his faith. The Pool of Siloam was at the southern end of the city, probably a considerable distance away, and so the

SOLID FOUNDATION BIBLE STUDIES

man, still blind, had to navigate through the city to the pool. He was obedient to Jesus, even if he did not understand the reasoning (v. 7).

The blind man continued to respond in faith after his healing. He testified to the truth he knew to his neighbors (vv. 8-12). He even spoke confidently when facing the hostile questioning of the Pharisees (vv. 13-17). His courage continued even as the interrogation grew more hostile and as his standing in the synagogue was at stake (vv. 24-34). Faith gives sight and lets us see clearly.

The blind man's parents limited their sight because of fear (9:18-23). His parents were not as courageous. Like most Jews, they were under the thumbs of the Pharisees. They were afraid they would be thrown out of the synagogue for saying too much. Excommunication had far-reaching effects on a Jew. It would mean banishment from social relationships as well as from religious rites.

These parents used their son as a shield to protect themselves and their social status. Their son could be excommunicated if *he* said that Jesus was the Christ. Their hands-off attitude put their own interests above their son's. They passed the buck.

The man's parents had an opportunity to know Jesus because of the testimony of their son and to obediently put their faith in Jesus. But it would take a bold decision. Jesus had taught that there were costs involved in following him (Matthew 8:18-22; 19:16-30; Luke 14:25-35). Fear limits sight. When out of fear we attempt to limit our risks, we may also limit our blessings.

The Pharisees refused sight because of pride (9:39-41). More and more people were following Jesus, and surely the Pharisees felt like they were losing control. Jesus was proving his claims about himself through the miracles he was performing. He spoke boldly to the Pharisees, challenging their narrow thinking. Even the temple guards were captivated by his teaching and would not arrest him (John 7:45-48).

How could the Pharisees continue to contend that Jesus was a fraud? They found two explanations. The first was to claim that miracles were not from God, but from Satan. The second was to deny that miracle occurred. They would argue that the man they saw was not really the one born blind but merely resembled him. Neither explanation was supported by the evidence, but that was irrelevant. Their pride forced them to be blind to the reality of the miracle.

Furthermore, their pride made them blind to their mission. Caring more about holding on to their own positions of authority than the well-being of the people they were called to lead, they treated others with contempt (vv. 28, 34).

Finally, the pride of the Pharisees made them blind to their own condition before God. Jesus told them that their arrogance left them in their guilt.

How do we respond to this miracle of Jesus? Do we, like the blind man, obey him in faith? When we do so we begin to see this world more clearly. Or do our fears cloud our vision, causing us to find excuses to avoid his call? Or worst of all, does our pride tempt us to refuse to acknowledge the reality of our sin? The choices are the same today as they were on that day long ago.

It's Greek to Me

After the Pharisees expelled the man from the synagogue, Jesus found him (v. 35). The word "found" in this verse is "heurisko" in the Greek. It means "to locate as a result of a search." It is the same word used by Jesus in Luke 15:3-7 for finding lost sheep. The good shepherd left the ninety-nine on a planned mission to find the one. This man had been kicked out of the temple, representing the Old Covenant sacrifices. Now, Jesus searched for him, and upon finding him, invited him to believe in him, the conveyor of the New Covenant. What a contrast of law and grace!

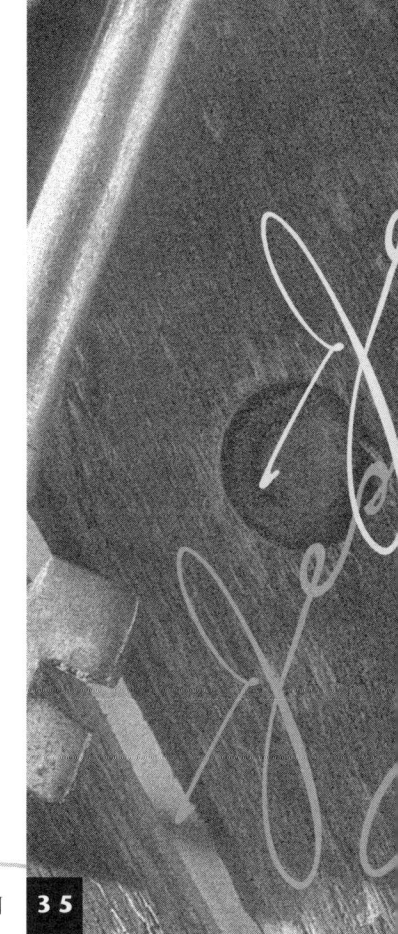

IN THE BEGINNING . . .

Use one of the following activities to help learners summarize the value of sight.

Blind Guide

Time: 10 minutes

Materials Needed
- two blindfolds

Before class, set up two columns of six chairs each. Each column should be identical, with about two feet between each chair in each column and about four feet separating the columns.

After all class members have arrived, ask for two pairs of volunteers for this contest. For each pair, assign one member to be the runner, the other to be the guide. Position each runner at the end of one of the columns of chairs. Have their guides blindfold them. At your signal, they will weave through their column of chairs without touching a chair. Their guides will lead them with verbal commands only. If a runner touches a chair, he must stand motionless for ten seconds before proceeding. The first runner successfully guided through the chairs wins the race.

After the contest, lead into today's Bible lesson by saying, **"The gift of sight is precious indeed. Without it, even the simplest tasks can be difficult.**

"In the ninth chapter of John, Jesus heals a man who had been blind since birth. This started a chain reaction of events as the Pharisees tried to deal with the popularity of Jesus. As we study this passage today, pay attention to the contrasts among some of the people involved. Jesus used this miracle as an opportunity to teach us about spiritual blindness."

Sight Unseen

Time: 10-12 minutes

Materials Needed
- chalkboard, chalk

When everyone has arrived, turn out the lights in the room. Pull the blinds on any windows and close doors to make the room as dark as possible. Then say, **"I want you to try to imagine what it would feel like to live with blindness. Imagine, if you can, being an adult who has lived your entire life without ever seeing the world around you. You have never seen the clouds on a summer day or the stars at night. You've never experienced red or purple. Take a few moments just to try to imagine what your world might be like."**

After several moments, turn the lights back on and ask people to meet in groups of three to discuss how they imagine life without sight. Write the following questions on the chalkboard:

- **What would you miss being able to see? Why?**
- **What activities that you enjoy now would be impossible or limited?**
- **How would your condition affect your relationships with others?**

SOLID FOUNDATION BIBLE STUDIES

Give groups two to three minutes to discuss these questions, and then bring them back together. Ask them to give some of the responses to the questions as you write them on the chalkboard.

Lead into today's lesson by saying, **"One of the things we can take for granted in life is our sight. Without it, our lives would be profoundly different.**

"In the ninth chapter of John, Jesus heals a man who had been blind since birth. This started a chain reaction of events as the Pharisees tried to deal with the popularity of Jesus. As we study this passage today, pay attention to the contrasts among some of the people involved. Jesus used this miracle as an opportunity to teach us about spiritual blindness."

THE WORD . . .

Use one of the following activities to help students compare and contrast ways that people reacted to the healing of the blind man.

Unfolding the Drama

Time: 25-30 minutes

Get most or many of your class members involved in reading John 9. As class begins, ask volunteers to read different parts in this account: disciple(s), Jesus, blind man, neighbors (two to four), Pharisees (three or more), parents. You assume the role of the narrator and read everything in the passage that is not a direct quote. Pause as you read to allow assigned students to read their parts.

After the Scripture is read, distribute copies of the "Compare and Contrast" worksheet. Instruct participants to follow the directions on the sheet. If your class works better in teams, you may divide the class into groups of about six people each and have the groups work together on this project. As students work, move among them to give help as needed. Refer to the **Scripture Commentary** and the suggested responses below as necessary. While there is no right or wrong response to each question, encourage students to be able to explain their answers.

1. **Choose a key quote from each person/group that best reveals his/their character.**
   - **the blind man** *"I was blind, but now I see!"; "He is a prophet."*
   - **his parents** *"He is of age; ask him."*
   - **the Pharisees** *"What? Are we blind too?" "How dare you lecture us!"*
2. **Describe one action taken by each person/group that best reveals his/their motives.**
   - **the blind man** *He went to the pool and washed; he stood up to the Pharisees.*
   - **his parents** *They avoided taking a stand when asked about the miracle.*
   - **the Pharisees** *They criticized Jesus for healing on the Sabbath; they expelled the man from the synagogue.*

Materials Needed

↣ *copies of the worksheet from page 41, pens or pencils*

3. **Label the attitude of each person/group in a single word.**
   - **the blind man** *obedient, trusting*
   - **his parents** *fearful, spineless*
   - **the Pharisees** *arrogant, proud, tyrannical*
4. **What title should be given this story if we were to consider each person/group to be the main character(s)?**
   - **the blind man** *Eyes of Faith; Trust and Obey*
   - **his parents** *We Know Nothing!*
   - **the Pharisees** *Don't Confuse Us With Facts, Our Minds Are Made Up*

After work has been completed, allow individuals or groups to share answers with the class as a whole. Make sure they explain thoroughly. Comment as necessary. Then close this activity with words similar to these: **"How do we respond to this miracle of Jesus? Do we, like the blind man, obey him in faith? When we do so, we begin to see this world more clearly. Or do our fears, like those of his parents, cloud our vision, causing us to find excuses to avoid his call? Or worst of all, does pride like that of the Pharisees tempt us to stubbornly refuse to acknowledge the reality of our sin? The choices are the same today as they were on that day long ago."**

Mind Reading
Time: 25-30 minutes

Materials Needed
- *paper and markers*

Divide the class into three groups. Give each group several pieces of plain paper and a marker. Each group will be assigned a person or people from John 9. As they read the chapter, they should concentrate upon the person or people they have been assigned and try to imagine the unspoken thoughts they may have had during the story. They are to write at least three of those thoughts on paper. Ask them to write each thought in large letters on a separate piece of paper.

Group assignments and possible thoughts follow:

Group 1—The blind man *I don't understand this, but I'll try anything (v. 7); How dense can these guys be? (v. 26); I am so grateful to this man (v. 38).*

Group 2—The disciples, the neighbors, the parents *What is he going to do now? (vv. 3-5); This can't be true! (v. 8); We can get ourselves in trouble if we say too much (vv. 18, 19).*

Group 3—The Pharisees *We've got to discredit this man Jesus (v. 16); How dare this filthy pig treat us this way! (v. 34); He is making us look like fools again (v. 41).*

As groups work, move among them to help as necessary. Refer to the **Scripture Commentary** and the suggested responses to help you. Encourage imagination and creativity.

When group work is complete, have a representative from each group bring its signs to the front of the room. Read John 9 slowly. As you come to a section in which one of the characters is mentioned, the group member should hold up the sign containing the thought that character may have had at that point in the story. After you finish reading, allow the class to discuss any of the thoughts mentioned. Comment as necessary for completeness and clarity.

Close with these ideas: **"What are we thinking when confronted with this miracle of Jesus? Do we, like the blind man, obey him in faith? When we do so, we begin to see this world more clearly. Or do our fears, like those of his parents, cloud our vision, causing us to find excuses to avoid his call? Or worst of all, does pride like that of the Pharisees tempt us to stubbornly refuse to acknowledge the reality of our sin? The choices are the same today as they were on that day long ago."**

THE WORD BECAME FLESH . . .

Use one of the following activities to help students respond in specific ways to the vision God gives them as Christians.

Case Studies

Time: 10-15 minutes

Allow the class to group in pairs or triads. Give a copy of the case studies to each group. Have them select one of the two cases and consider possible responses of the main characters. How could they react with the faith of the blind man? How could they react with the fear of the parents? How could they react with the arrogance of the Pharisees?

Move among groups as they work. Remind them of the three reactions seen in today's text. Encourage them to think of possible reactions of the characters in the case studies that would be similar. Refer to the following suggested answers to help if needed.

Case 1

Jeff and Maureen could react in faith like the blind man. They could examine the faith of their children and thank Jesus for the change he made in them. They could tell others about the new-found faith of their family.

Jeff and Maureen could react in fear like the blind man's parents. Knowing that being "too religious" was just not acceptable in their social circles, they could brush off the change in their kids with patronizing remarks. "I guess they found something that works for them. We've always raised them to make their own decisions."

They could react in pride like the Pharisees. They could let their children know that their fanaticism was an embarrassment and openly criticize their newfound beliefs.

Case 2

Doug could react in faith like the blind man. He could talk to Nancy to learn more about this God who makes the broken whole.

He could react in fear like the parents. This religious thing was just a bit scary. What if it didn't work for him? Could he handle any more disappointments in his life?

He could react in pride like the Pharisees. How dare anyone interfere with his life! How could they possibly know the pain he has known!

Materials Needed

- copies of the case studies on page 42 for every two or three students

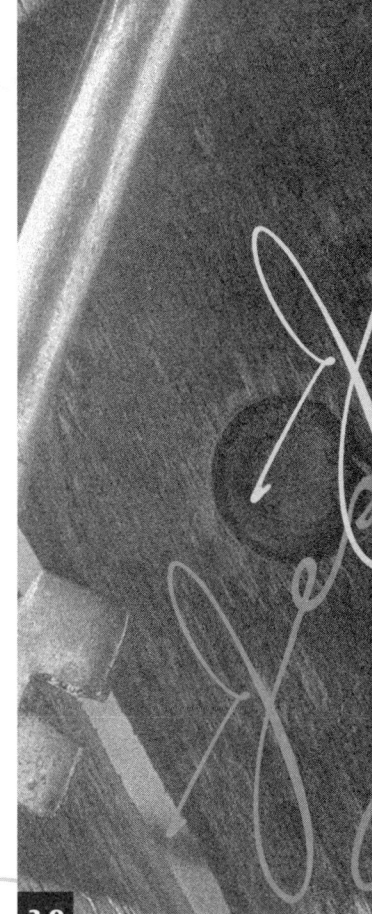

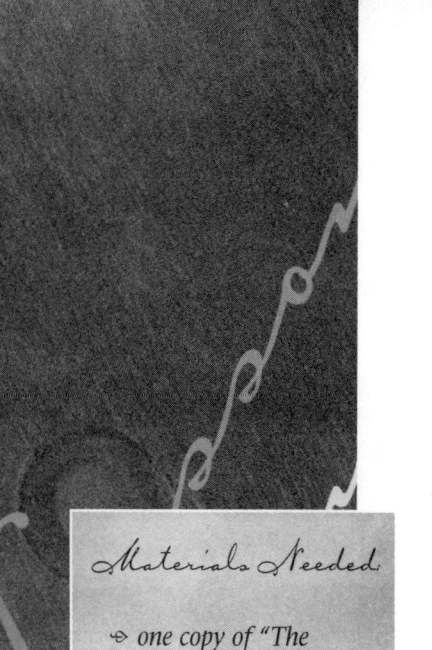

Close with words like these, **"The Pharisees had one big blind spot. They were right in their own eyes and did not want to be challenged. The blind man's parents were fearful and didn't want to risk any change in their lives. The blind man responded to Jesus by faith and with boldness in his testimony. We all know people who face the same choices. We all face those choices ourselves. How can we respond?"**

Close in prayer, praising Jesus for who he is and what he is doing in the lives of your class.

The Follow-Through Factor

Time: 5 minutes

This section appears in every lesson in this series. This weekly devotion plan helps class members apply the Bible study throughout the coming week. You may use it immediately after the Bible study or in conjunction with the preceding activity.

Give each person a copy of the handout. Take time to briefly read through it, but do not discuss any of the questions at this time.

Close the session in prayer.

NOTES

Materials Needed

• one copy of "The Follow-Through Factor" handout from page 43 for each person

SOLID FOUNDATION BIBLE STUDIES

COMPARE & CONTRAST

Answer the questions below for each person or group of people.

1. **Choose a key quote from each person/group that best reveals his/their character.**
   - **the blind man**
   - **his parents**
   - **the Pharisees**

2. **Describe one action taken by each person/group that best reveals his/their motives.**
   - **the blind man**
   - **his parents**
   - **the Pharisees**

3. **Label the attitude of each person/group in a single word.**
   - **the blind man**
   - **his parents**
   - **the Pharisees**

4. **What title should be given this story if we were to consider each person/group to be the main character(s)?**
   - **the blind man**
   - **his parents**
   - **the Pharisees**

LESSON 4

CASE STUDIES

Case 1—Kids Today!

Jeff and Maureen Smythe have never been terribly religious. They are nominal members of First Church and attend on Easter and Christmas Eve. Likewise, their friends and Jeff's colleagues in state government have a distant respect mixed with skepticism concerning God. A little religion is one's civic duty, but taking church too seriously should be treated with suspicion.

The Smythes' kids had extremely rebellious years as early teens. Jeff and Maureen knew that they had experimented with alcohol and drugs and had acted out sexually. But in the past few months they have started attending church with friends. They claim to have "come to know Jesus as Savior." This type of thinking is foreign to the Smythes, but they see a remarkable change in the lives of their children. Their question is, how should they react to the faith of their children?

Case 2—Crutch or Cure?

Doug has been confined to a wheelchair for the past ten years. As a teen his car was hit by a drunk driver, leaving him paralyzed from the waist down and bitter from the neck up. His dreams of fulfilling his promise as a professional athlete were dashed. He has distanced himself from people and lived a modest life in his parents' home, making do with a disability check from the insurance company.

Nancy is the only friend from high school that hasn't deserted him. But he has no idea why she hasn't. He treats her with the same bitterness he aims at the rest of the world. Lately he read a book she left for him. It was an autobiography of a young woman who suffered a similar injury. She had turned to a faith in Jesus and was now living a productive life of joy. Doug knows Nancy will want to discuss this book. How would he respond?

SOLID FOUNDATION BIBLE STUDIES

THE FOLLOW-THROUGH FACTOR
Jesus frees us from our blind spots.

Consider the implications of your last Bible study through this next week.

Monday
Read John 9:1-5 and Romans 8:28-39.
According to these passages, why does God sometimes allow suffering? What promises has God given you for going through difficult times? Thank him today for his promises in the midst of difficulties.

Tuesday
Read John 9:8-11 and 1 Peter 3:13-16.
Like the man born blind, we are living testimonies of God's work in the world. List several ways that God is blessing you that you could share naturally with a friend.

Wednesday
Read John 9:20-23 and Luke 14:25-35.
There are costs involved in following Jesus. The parents decided the costs were too high; their son paid the price but received an even greater reward. What costs are you not willing to make to follow Jesus in every area of your life?

Thursday
Read John 9:24-29 and 1 John 5:13-20.
What did the Pharisees "know"?
What did they not "know"?
What did the man born blind "know"?
What is important for us to know?

Friday
Read John 9:30-33 and James 5:13-18.
Who does God listen to? Take an extended time in prayer today for the needs of your church, especially its leadership.

Saturday
Read John 9:35-38 and Psalm 100.
How are knowledge (Psalm 100:3), belief (John 9:38), and worship connected? In preparation for worship tomorrow, take time to worship God for who he is and what he is doing in your life, the life of your family, and the life of your church.

LESSON 4

LESSON 5
Jesus frees us from our fear of death

Lesson Objectives

In the course of this lesson, students will be able to
- *describe a great fear.*
- *list ways the fear of death limited the disciples, Mary and Martha, and the leaders of the Jews.*
- *consider how personal fears of death are limiting.*

LESSON SCRIPTURE
John 11:1-57

SCRIPTURE COMMENTARY

Commenting upon carnal man, philosopher Thomas Hobbes observed, "No arts, no letters, no society, and which is worst of all, *continual fear and danger of violent death,* and the life of man is solitary, poor, nasty, brutish, and short." (Emphasis added.)

Fear of death is as crippling as the object of that fear. In John 11 we see the three different groups of people reacting to the fear of death. We also see a powerful miracle that assures us that, in Jesus, such fear is baseless.

Fear of death can make us hesitant to walk with Jesus (11:1-16). The disciples must have been perplexed when Jesus did not immediately rush to the side of Lazarus upon hearing of his friend's illness (vv. 1-6). But they quite probably were relieved. It was safer to remain where they were than to go where people were waiting to stone Jesus and probably his followers as well (v. 8)!

Bafflement must have been mixed with their anxiety when, after waiting two more days, Jesus said, "Let us go back to Judea" (v. 7). It seemed absurd to them; it was a suicide mission. Even after three years of traveling with the Master, their fear of death led to doubt. Fear of death made them hesitant to continue walking with Jesus.

Jesus answered their fears with a short proverb. He encouraged the disciples that as long as one "walks by day" (in the light provided by Jesus) nothing could harm them (11:9). One stumbles when "he has no light," separated from the Savior (v. 10).

Still they did not understand. When Jesus said that Lazarus had fallen "asleep," the disciples breathed a sigh of relief. Sleep would give him the rest he needed to heal. They had a good excuse to stay where it was relatively safe. Jesus needed to explain his euphemism. Lazarus had died. But the death of Jesus' friend would provide a way to bolster the disciples' fear-ravaged faith (vv. 11-15).

Only analytical Thomas responded in faith to Jesus. Granted, Thomas's statement was uttered with a sigh of resignation, but he was beginning to understand. Even dying with Jesus was to be preferred to living without him (v. 16).

Fear of death can make us doubt what we know about Jesus (11:17-44). Martha and Mary knew Jesus well. Earlier in his ministry, Martha had been impressed with him and invited him into their home. At that time Mary had dropped everything just to sit and listen to his teachings (Luke 10:38, 39). They had every opportunity to know him as a man of wisdom, power, and compassion.

Yet in the face of death, doubt emerged. Martha ran to Jesus and asked, in effect, "Where were you? Why did you let us down?" She knew Jesus was only about one day away, but it took him four days to arrive. Where was his wisdom? Where was his compassion? Yet, even in tragedy a thread of faith remained (vv. 17-22).

It may have sounded like a religious platitude when Jesus responded, "Your brother will rise again." Martha was thinking merely of the resurrection that will happen at Jesus' second coming. Surely she had heard Jesus speak about this resurrection. Jesus assured her in her grief that the power of that resurrection was present at that moment (vv. 23-27). Before Jesus raised Lazarus, he raised Martha.

Mary ran to Jesus and used the same words as her sister. Nevertheless, if Martha's words had overtones of anger and confrontation, Mary's words and actions implied hopelessness and surrender. She fell at his feet in tears (vv. 28-36).

Jesus addressed their fears and doubts in bold fashion. "Take away the stone," he ordered. But Martha hesitated. As the older sister in the family, it was her responsibility to authorize moving of the stone. Her first thought was practical. After four days in the hot Judean climate, the smell in the cave would be noxious. Jesus called on the faith that she had previously professed in him. "Did I not tell you . . . you would see the glory of God" (v. 40).

Fear of death can lead us to question everything we know about Jesus. The raising of Lazarus brings us out of despair and underlines facts we have already accepted.

Fear of death can cause us to betray Jesus (11:45-57). This miracle had an interesting by-product. Amazingly, after witnessing a man being resurrected from the dead, some felt the need to tell the authorities rather than rejoice in the extraordinary. Fear caused them to betray Jesus (vv. 45, 46).

Nowhere in this account do we see the Pharisees and chief priests denying the reality of this miracle. But they did not and could not surrender to the implications of it. Instead of seeing Jesus as the one who could save them from death, a new fear was ignited. Since Jesus displayed undeniable power, he would be accepted as the Messiah. Since popular opinion was that the Messiah would throw off Roman rule, Caesar would see him as a threat and crush his rebellion. Therefore, the existence of their nation and their very lives were threatened (vv. 47, 48).

The twisted logic of fear gave birth to a plan. One man was threatening the lives of everyone in Israel. For that reason, it was necessary for that man to die to avoid the judgment that would come upon them. (vv. 49-57).

Fear of death destroys human life. Because they feared death, the apostles were hesitant to continue to walk with Jesus. Because they feared death, Mary and Martha began to doubt the power and love of Jesus. Because they feared death, the Jewish leaders tried to do away with Jesus. These reactions continue to the present day. But also continuing is the testimony of the One who conquers death, both for himself and for anyone who lives in allegiance to him.

Further Insight

Jesus responded to people in ways that met the needs of their personalities. Martha, the "thinker," and Mary, "the feeler," came to Jesus with identical concerns phrased in identical words (vv. 21, 32). Yet Jesus answered them differently. To Martha he offered words of assurance. He reasoned with her, helping her recall both the facts of Scripture and the details of his ministry (vv. 23-27). In the case of Mary, he quietly moved to Lazarus' grave site and had a good cry with her (vv. 33-35). When we meet people in crisis, we must do likewise. Instead of pat answers, we need to communicate truth in a manner that meets the needs of their personalities.

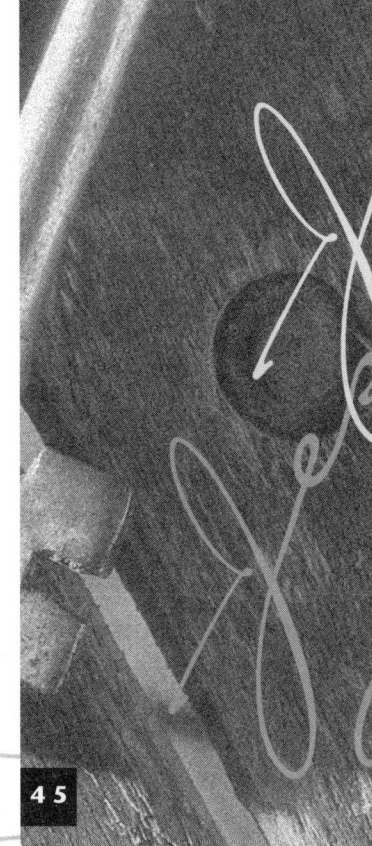

IN THE BEGINNING...

Use one of the following activities to help learners describe a great fear.

Top Ten Fears

Time: 10-15 minutes

Materials Needed
- chalkboard, chalk

Begin class with a rapid-fire brainstorming session. Write the numerals from one to twenty down the left side of the chalkboard. Ask for a volunteer with a watch to be your timekeeper. The remainder of the class will try to list twenty fears in sixty seconds. On the timekeeper's signal, they will call out those fears as fast as you can write them. Continue until the list is complete or time is called. Never pause to comment on responses while brainstorming is in progress.

Then say, **"Now let's narrow this list down to the 'Top Ten Fears' that people face. Which of the fears we listed should definitely be included?"**

Circle the responses that the class agrees should be in the top ten. Then, with the class's help, number them from one to ten, one being the biggest fear most people face.

Look at where death was placed on the list. Move into the Bible study by asking, **"Why do people fear death? Does a fear of death bring about more fears? How does a fear of death affect behavior?"** (Pause for responses.)

"Death seems to be a universal fear. It is a fear that is the root of many other fears. It is also a fear that greatly affects the behavior of people. Let us look at how three different groups of people in John 11 responded to their fears of death."

Word Compass

Time: 10-15 minutes

Materials Needed
- copies of the puzzle from page 51 for all students

As students arrive, give them a copy of the word compass puzzle. To solve the puzzle, they will begin with the circled letter. They should then follow the directions on the compass to find the remaining letters of a famous quote. They need to record the letters in the blanks below. The first word is done for them.

After all have arrived and most, if not all, have solved the puzzle, ask for the solution. The quote should read, *The only thing we have to fear is fear itself* (Franklin Delano Roosevelt).

Begin a class discussion with these questions: **"What is meant by this familiar quote? Is this statement true or false? Why?"** Allow students to discuss this for a few minutes, and then ask, **"What real fears do people have? What do you think is the greatest fear that most people in the world today have?"**

The class may agree that death is that great fear. If not, ask, **"What about death? Does a fear of death bring about more fears? How does fear of death affect people's behavior?"**

Segue into the Bible lesson with these words: **"Death seems to be a universal fear. It is a fear that is the root of many other fears. It is also a fear that greatly affects the behavior of people. Let us look at how three different groups of people in John 11 responded to their fears of death."**

THE WORD . . .

Use one of the following activities to help students list ways the fear of death limited the disciples, Mary and Martha, and the leaders of the Jews.

Character Analysis

Time: 30-35 minutes

Divide the class into three groups. Assign each group one of the following groups of characters from John 11. If groups have more than five or six in them, assign additional groups.

Group 1—The disciples	**John 11:1-16**
Group 2—Mary and Martha	**John 11:17-44**
Group 3—The chief priests and the Pharisees	**John 11:45-57**

Ask each group to read its assigned section of the lesson text and analyze the characters with the questions listed below.

As groups work, move among them to help them with their analyses as necessary. Refer to the **Scripture Commentary** and suggested responses below for additional help.

1. **What specifically did they fear?**
   - **The disciples**

     The disciples feared the Jews in Judea would kill Jesus and them.

   - **Mary and Martha**

     Jesus did not respond as quickly to the news of Lazarus's illness as they thought he would. Therefore, Mary and Martha probably feared that Jesus was either not as loving or as powerful as they had believed.

   - **The chief priests and the Pharisees**

     The leaders feared that the raising of Lazarus would convince the people to accept Jesus as their king. They feared that this would cause Rome to respond by attacking Judea to crush the rebellion.

2. **How did fear affect behavior?**
   - **The disciples**

     The disciples probably seriously questioned whether they should continue to follow Jesus.

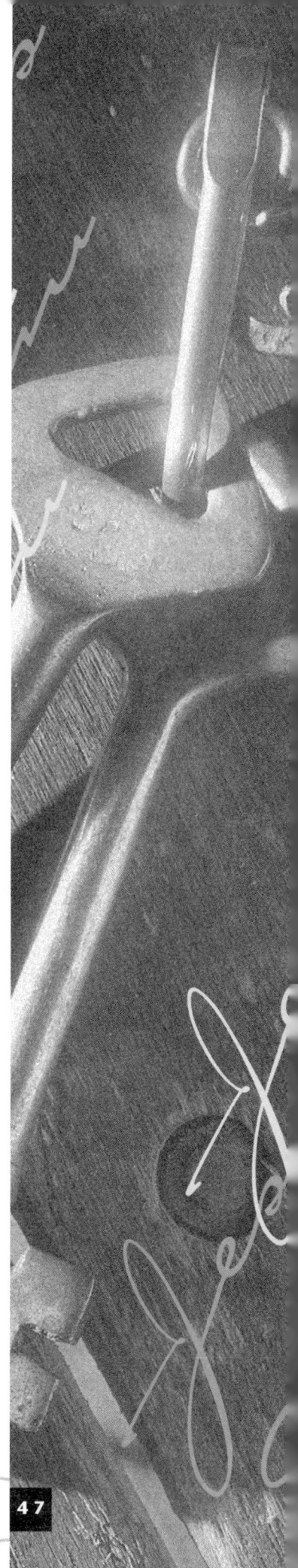

- **Mary and Martha**

  Mary and Martha continued to mourn for the loss of their brother even though Jesus was with them.

- **The chief priests and the Pharisees**

  The chief priests and the Pharisees treated Jesus as a threat and looked for an opportunity to kill him.

3. What did they need to understand about Jesus' power over death?

- **The disciples**

  No one can take the life of a disciple of Jesus. We are secure and protected for eternity in him.

- **Mary and Martha**

  Jesus has full authority over death now. He will use that power in the way that is best for those who trust him.

- **The chief priests and the Pharisees**

  The taking of Jesus' life was not the end, but the beginning of a reign that would last forever.

After the groups are finished, allow each group to give a brief report about its discussion. Comment as necessary for clarity and completeness. Close with these words: **"Each of these groups feared death. With each of these fears came a negative response in their behavior. The disciples feared death by the hands of the Jews, making them reluctant to follow Jesus to Judea. Mary and Martha feared that Jesus' love somehow stopped at death, making them doubt his power and compassion. The leaders feared that Jesus' popularity would lead to an attack by Rome and cause the death of their nation. Therefore, they plotted his death. Does fear of death limit us in similar ways today?"**

Acrostic Poetry

Time: 25-30 minutes

Divide the class into three teams. Assign each team one of the following groups of characters from John 11.

Group 1—The disciples	**John 11:1-16**
Group 2—Mary and Martha	**John 11:17-44**
Group 3—The chief priests and the Pharisees	**John 11:45-57**

Distribute pens, paper, and copies of the **Scripture Commentary** to each team. Ask each team to read its assigned section of the lesson text and create an acrostic poem. Each line of the poem begins with one of the letters of the phrase, "FEAR OF DEATH" and the total poem should reflect how that group of characters reacted to Jesus because of their fear.

As groups work, move among them to help them with their poetry as necessary. The sample poems which follow may help.

Materials Needed

↝ *paper, pens, copies of the Scripture Commentary*

The disciples	Mary and Martha	Chief priests and Pharisees
Followers	**F**orlorn because we	**F**ighting God, we
Eager to lead	**E**xpect	**E**ventually turn to ourselves
And	**A** saving God to	**A**lone for
Reluctant to die	**R**espond to our timetable, we	**R**edemption.
Often	**O**verlook what we know,	**O**ur response to his
Face a	**F**orget what we have experienced, and	**F**antastic acts is to
Dilemma.	**D**oubt what we have seen.	**D**espise his
Either fear	**E**nter the Savior,	**E**ntrance into a world we wish to control,
And shrink back, or	**A**nd we watch as he	**A**nd we attempt
Trust and	**T**riumphs over the	**T**o silence
Head forward with the Master.	**H**arsh reality of death.	**H**im.

Adapt It

If your class enjoys reading poetry more than writing it, this activity is easily adapted. Write these three poems on poster board. Do not title them. Assign groups the sections of Scripture above and ask them to match a poem with the main characters of each section.

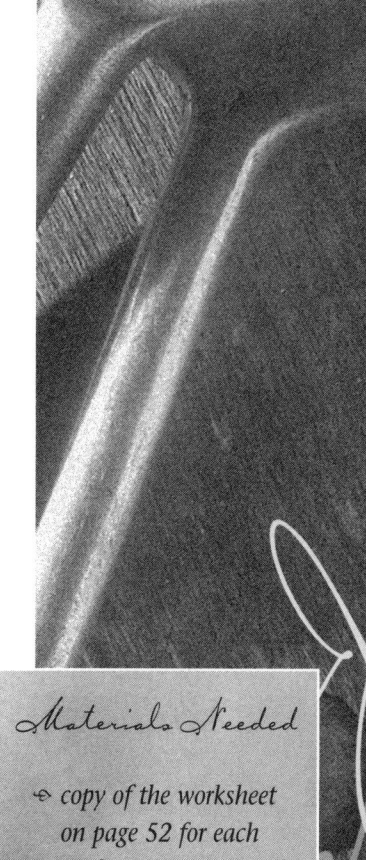

After the groups are finished, allow each group to read and explain its poem. Comment as necessary for clarity and completeness. Close with these words: **"Each of these groups feared death. The disciples feared death by the hands of the Jews, making them reluctant to follow Jesus to Judea. Mary and Martha feared that Jesus' love somehow stopped at death, making them doubt his power and compassion. The leaders feared that Jesus' popularity would lead to an attack by Rome and the cause the death of their nation. Therefore, they plotted his death. Does fear of death limit us in similar ways today?"**

THE WORD BECAME FLESH . . .

Use one of the following activities to help students consider how personal fears of death are limiting.

Self-Evaluation

Time: 10-15 minutes

Distribute a copy of the self-evaluation form to each student. By circling a number from one to five, each student is to indicate to what extent he or she identifies with each "fear statement." A response of one means, "I'm not like this at all," and five means, "I am exactly like this." On the bottom half of the page, they are to pick the area in which they have the highest score and make a list of ways they believe that they need to change.

When all have completed their charts, have class members turn to a partner to explain their responses. Close by asking these pairs of students to pray that the power and love of Jesus will overcome their fears of death.

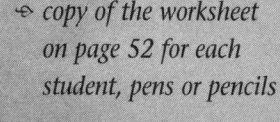

Materials Needed

- *copy of the worksheet on page 52 for each student, pens or pencils*

FREE INDEED

Materials Needed

◈ one copy of "The Follow-Through Factor" handout from page 53 for each person

The Follow-Through Factor
Time: 5 minutes

This section appears in every lesson in this series. This weekly devotion plan helps class members apply the Bible study throughout the coming week. You may use it immediately after the Bible study or in conjunction with the preceding activity.

Give each person a copy of the handout. Take time to briefly read through it, but do not discuss any of the questions at this time.

Close the session in prayer.

NOTES

WORD COMPASS

To solve the Word Compass puzzle, begin with the circled letter. Then follow the directions on the compass to find the remaining letters of a famous quote. Record the letters in the blanks below. The first word is done for you. From the circled letter "T" we traveled south four spaces to the letter "H." From there, we traveled two spaces west for the letter "E." Take it from there!

NORTH

N	E	R	L	I	A
F	F	(T)	O	S	E
O	I	E	W	H	H
T	E	L	Y	S	T
I	A	F	T	R	E
E	N	H	G	A	V

WEST   **EAST**

SOUTH

T H E
— — — — — — —   — — — — —
   4S 2W   3N 2N 3E 3S   2E 1N 4W 3S 2E

— —   — — — —   — —
3N 1W   2E 3S 1E 1N   2W 3N

— — — —   — —   — — — —
3W 5E 1N 3W   2E 1S   3W 1N 4S 3E

— — — — — —
4W 1N 4E 3W 1E 1S

Franklin Delano Roosevelt, First Inaugural Address (March 4, 1933)

LESSON 5   51

SELF-EVALUATION

Read each statement below. Circle a number from one to five to indicate to what extent you identify with each statement. A response of one means, "I'm not like this at all," and five means, "I am exactly like this." After completing the evaluation, pick the area in which you have the highest score. One the bottom half of the page, make a list of ways you believe that you need to change.

1. I am hesitant to speak of my faith for fear of being "embarrassed to death."   1   2   3   4   5

2. I doubt that I could be a strong Christian, if I feared that I could be killed for my faith.   1   2   3   4   5

3. The sudden death of a loved one could make me doubt that Jesus really loves me.   1   2   3   4   5

4. The sudden death of a loved one could make me doubt that Jesus really gives victory over death.   1   2   3   4   5

5. I fear that being truly committed to Jesus could be the death of my way of life.   1   2   3   4   5

6. I could see myself betraying Jesus because I am afraid of "dying to self."   1   2   3   4   5

I can see that my fear of death can cause me to _____
_____
_____
_____

For that reason I need to _____
_____
_____
_____

SOLID FOUNDATION BIBLE STUDIES

THE FOLLOW-THROUGH FACTOR
Jesus frees us from our fear of death.

Consider the implications of your last Bible study through this next week.

Monday
Read John 11:9, 10; John 1:4, 5; 3:19-21; 8:12; 9:5; 12:35, 36.
  In what three areas of your life are you walking in the light?
  In what three areas are you walking in darkness?

Tuesday
Read John 11:21-23; 32-35 and Psalm 10.
  If you feel like God is far away when you pray about a certain aspect of your life, what is it? Take time in prayer to be completely honest with God. If you are frustrated, tell him so. If you are wondering why he seems far away, ask him why.

Wednesday
Read John 11:25-27 and John 1:4; 14:6.
  How do these words comfort you?
  Prayerfully thank God for his provision of life. Looking forward to the resurrection when Jesus returns, praise God for his grace.

Thursday
Read John 11:32; Luke 10:38-42; and John 12:1-3.
  What does Mary's physical position in relation to Jesus say about her heart?
  Surrender yourself to Jesus. Whatever you are holding back from him, give over to him.

Friday
Read John 11:33-36; Hebrews 4:14-16; and Romans 12:15.
  Why can you approach God's throne with confidence?
  With whom can you mourn? How can you help to bring hope?

Saturday
Read John 11:38-45 and Revelation 15:3, 4.
  In what area of your life this weekend can you give glory to God?
  Take time to worship God today, using the words of Revelation 15:3, 4.

LESSON 5

LESSON 6

Jesus frees us from our past mistakes.

Lesson Objectives

In the course of this lesson, students will be able to
- *recall a time when they were able to make a fresh start.*
- *summarize the story of Peter's fresh start after denying Jesus.*
- *decide to make a fresh start in his or her relationship with God in a particular area of life.*

LESSON SCRIPTURE
John 21:1-23

SCRIPTURE COMMENTARY

"I'd like to get away from earth awhile/And then come back to it and begin over," wrote the great American poet Robert Frost ("Birches"). Certainly Peter would have desired such an opportunity after he denied three times even knowing Jesus. In John 21 Peter was given that chance to start over.

Jesus' call to us is unchanged over time (John 21:1-14; Luke 5:1-11). Even though Jesus had risen from the dead, Peter still felt anguish. He decided to go fishing. Perhaps he was saying, "I have failed in following Jesus. I'm going back to what I know." So Peter went out in a boat with Thomas, Nathanael, James, John, and two other disciples. All night they fished and caught nothing.

Suddenly the fishermen heard a voice from the shore. It told them to throw the net on the right side of the boat, that there they would find some fish. The disciples tugged in the empty net and threw it on the other side. The net filled with so many fish that they couldn't pull them back in. *Deja vu*. It was another miracle, reminding them of the time when Jesus had first called them (Luke 5:1-11).

This time Peter swam to Jesus rather than falling to his knees. He jumped from the boat to get to Jesus while the rest watched from the boat. And yet Peter did give some thought to his actions before jumping this time. Jewish custom held that greeting someone is a religious act which required people to be fully clothed. So Peter stopped to put on his outer cloak before diving.

When Peter came ashore, Jesus had a fire burning with fish on it and some bread. What a powerful scene! Peter was reassured in this act that nothing had changed. Despite what he had done, Jesus continued to call him to fellowship with him.

Jesus' forgiveness is always as great as our sin (John 21:15-17; John 13:34-38). Jesus wanted to forgive, to restore, and also to refocus. "Simon, son of John, do you truly love me more than these?"

If Jesus pointed to the fish and equipment as he said "more than these," he may have been telling Peter and the rest, "I want your passion to be on fishing for men, not fishing for fish." If Jesus pointed to the other disciples as he said "more than

SOLID FOUNDATION BIBLE STUDIES

these," he may have been admonishing Peter in another way. Peter was the first to the empty grave and out of the boat. No one else had made such a passionate profession of Jesus as Peter had (Matthew 16:16). But not one of Jesus' other disciples (except Judas) had treated Jesus so badly. Jesus said, in essence, "In light of the fact that you, of all people, did deny me, what are your affections toward me now?"

Peter's response was simply and humbly, "Yes, Lord, you know that I love you." No comparisons. No self-sufficiency. No foot in the mouth. He had learned through his errors and repentance the importance of servanthood and teamwork.

Peter was grieved by Jesus' threefold question. Three times Peter had denied Jesus (John 18:15-18, 25-27). Now, Jesus, in his loving forgiveness, gave Peter the chance to wipe out the memory of his three denials with three declarations of love. This was for the sake of both Peter and the rest of the disciples. In each instance, Peter's leadership was reconfirmed by Jesus. There could be no doubt left in anyone's mind that Peter would still take a leadership role in the early church, which came to fruition on the Day of Pentecost. Yet Peter's leadership, like Jesus', was to be that of a servant: "Follow me!" Jesus' forgiveness is always as great as our sin.

Jesus' plan for us will continue to be challenging (John 21:18-23). Peter's confession of his love for Jesus brought about a call to action. Jesus had said earlier, "I tell you the truth, anyone who has faith in me will do what I have been doing" (John 14:12). As the incarnation of the Father here on earth, Jesus came in a human body to reconcile a lost world to God. As the second incarnation, the Body of Christ, the church, has the same mission. "And he has committed to us the message of reconciliation. We are therefore Christ's ambassadors, as though God were making his appeal through us" (2 Corinthians 5:19, 20).

Jesus' challenging call to follow him also implied the kind of death Peter would face. Peter was crucified about 30 years after this. Peter believed it was such an honor to "follow Christ" in this way that he requested to be crucified upsidedown, considering himself unworthy to die in the same manner as his master.

As Christians, we are called to "follow Jesus" in the same ways. His mission is our mission. His passion for lost people should be our passion. We may be persecuted for our faith as he and the disciples were. We may even be called to give up our life for his sake, as most of the disciples did.

Only one of Jesus' apostles did not die a martyr's death, history tells us—the apostle John. Much speculation surrounding how he was to die started soon after Jesus' ascension. What did Jesus mean by his question, "If I want him to remain alive until I return, what is that to you?" Regardless of the interpretation, however, Jesus was telling Peter, and us, "Mind your own business! Don't concern yourself with how I will bless someone else. Just focus on this one thing: Follow me!"

Jesus gives all who wear his name a chance to start over. He continues to call us to action, as he has from the beginning. He is able to forgive us regardless of our sin. Finally, he renews his commission to us, trusting us with the greatest challenge any have known. He calls us to be his disciples and to make disciples of all nations.

It's Greek to Me

Many have noted that Jesus used the Greek word for love, "agapao" (love supremely with the entire self, including the will) in his first two questions and Peter answered with "phileo" (to like, approve of, sanction, treat affectionately). Phileo, however, is not necessarily a lower form of love than agapao, just more emotion-based. For Peter, especially, saying "yes, I phileo you," is a strong, emotional response to Jesus.

Another change in terminology concerns Jesus' response each time to Peter. In the first and third instances, he said to feed his lambs or sheep. The Greek word for feed used here is "bosko," to feed or keep. In the second instance, Jesus said, "Take care of my sheep." The Greek word for "take care of" is "poimaino," to tend a flock, nourish, care for, guide, defend. It is not enough just to "feed" people, to offer them the bread of life; it is also necessary for shepherds of God's flock to lead, guide, nurture, and defend them. Peter wrote to elders in 1 Peter 5:2, "Be shepherds (poimaino) of God's flock that is under your care."

IN THE BEGINNING...

Use one of the following activities to help learners recall a time when they were able to make a fresh start.

Sharing Breakout

Time: 10-12 minutes

Divide the class into groups of four or five people each. Each group should discuss a time in which they had a chance to start over.

Suggest the following areas: in a relationship, job, school, church, or health situation; or when they moved, married, or retired — or they can share in any other area they think of.

After groups are finished, lead a discussion with the entire class using these questions:

- How does it *feel* to get a fresh start in some area in your life?
- Imagine that you have really messed things up in some area of your life: a marriage or some other relationship or a job situation for instance. How would you react if the person whom you hurt gave you a fresh start? (You may need to start off the discussion on this question by sharing a brief story of your own.)

Lead into the Bible discussion by saying something like this: "**Our main character, the apostle Peter, was rough around the edges. The burly fisherman was courageous, yet impetuous; outgoing, yet unstable; faithful, yet disloyal. His foot often ended up in his mouth. He was an ordinary, flawed, human being like you and me. And yet he had the raw material with which Jesus could work. He was willing. He could be humbled. He had a tremendous heart for God and a passion for people. As he followed Jesus, Peter messed things up a number of times. Can you identify with him? Peter's biggest blunder, of course, was when he denied three times even knowing Jesus. Today, we'll look at Scripture to see how Jesus gives everyone a chance to start over."**

Life Is Amazing

Time: 8-10 minutes

Photocopy enough copies of the worksheet for each student. Copy half of the sheets on blue paper (or some other color) and the other half on yellow (or another color).

Shuffle the sheets so that the different colors will be handed out in random order. As you hand out the sheets to the class, make sure the sheets are upside-down. Instruct them to keep the sheets upsidedown until you signal them to begin.

Then explain: "**On the other side of your resource sheet is a maze. You will begin at the word 'Start' and work your way through this maze. There are only two rules you need to know. If you have a yellow sheet, you**

Materials Needed

- *copies of the maze on page 61 on two different colors of paper, pens, pencils*

SOLID FOUNDATION BIBLE STUDIES

are allowed to retrace your steps or start over any time you need to. If you have a blue sheet, you have one chance to get this right. You are not allowed to look ahead, and you cannot retrace your steps or start over. "

After everyone appears to have finished the maze (or gotten stuck, as the case may be), say, **"Life is sometimes like a maze, isn't it? Sometimes we run into dead ends. We often take wrong turns."** Ask, **"How is real life like your experience with this maze?"** Lead a brief discussion on this question. Then ask, **"How did you feel knowing that people around you could retrace their steps or start over again? For those of you who could retrace your steps or start over if you made a mistake, how did that feel?"**

Lead into the Bible discussion by saying something like this: **"Our main character, the apostle Peter, was rough around the edges. The burly fisherman was courageous, yet impetuous; outgoing, yet unstable; faithful, yet disloyal. His foot often ended up in his mouth. He was an ordinary, flawed, human being like you and me. And yet he had the raw material with which Jesus could work. He was willing. He could be humbled. He had a tremendous heart for God and a passion for people. As he followed Jesus, Peter messed things up a number of times. Can you identify with him? Peter's biggest blunder, of course, was when he denied three times even knowing Jesus. Today, we'll look at Scripture to see how Jesus gives everyone a chance to start over."**

THE WORD...

Use one of the following activities to enable students to summarize the story of Peter's fresh start after denying Jesus.

Bible Discussion Groups

Time: 20-25 minutes

Divide the class into at least three groups. (Groups should be no larger than 8 people.) You can use more than three groups by giving the same assignments to more than one group. You may read the Scripture, John 21:1-23, together as a class by asking three volunteers to read assigned sections (assign these before class), or have each group read the passage themselves.

After the Scripture passage has been read, give one of the following assignments to each of the groups. Give each group a copy of the **Scripture Commentary** to use.

Tell groups they are to study the passage with a particular topic in mind. Be sure each group has a facilitator, who will ask the questions and lead a discussion; a reporter, who will take notes on the discussion; a speaker, who will share what the

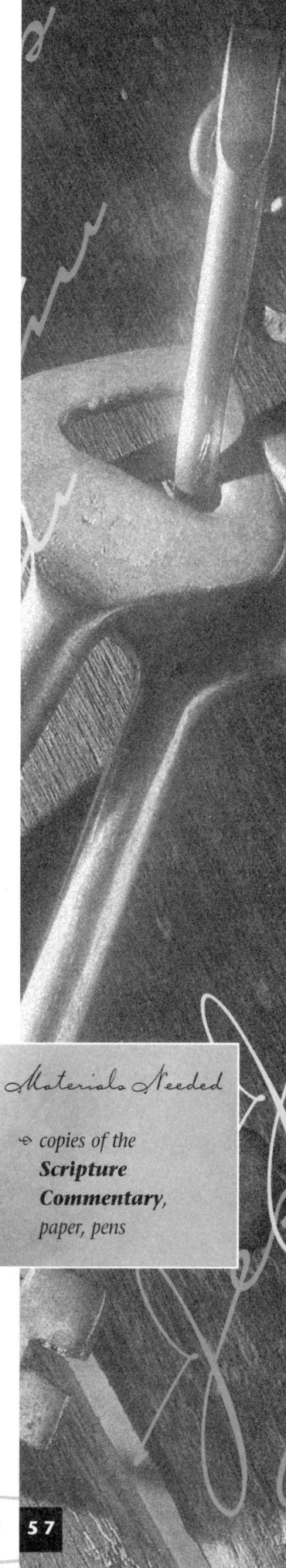

Materials Needed

- copies of the **Scripture Commentary**, paper, pens

group learned with the rest of the class; and possibly a timekeeper, who will assure the group finishes on time.

- **Group 1: Study the passage to learn how Jesus' power was displayed. Compare this passage with Luke 5:1-11. How did Jesus show his power in his ministry? Why did he display his power throughout his ministry? Where did his power come from? What miracles did Jesus perform in John 21? Why do you think Jesus performed these miracles?**

- **Group 2: Study the passage, looking particularly at Jesus' forgiveness. Also see John 13:34-38; Matthew 26:33; 16:16). Look at Matthew 16:16; 26:33. How did Peter's words line up with his actions? Why did Jesus ask Peter three times if he loved him? How did Jesus help Peter deal with his grief before moving forward to forgiveness? How was Jesus' forgiveness for Peter at least as great as Peter's sin? How are love and forgiveness related?**

- **Group 3: Study the passage to learn how Jesus has a challenging plan for each of us. Also see Mark 1:14-20; John 14:12; 2 Corinthians 5:19, 20. How did Jesus challenge Peter? How does forgiveness necessarily lead to action? What might Christians today face if they truly love Jesus and serve him? How are Christians called to be a blessing? How does being reconciled to God challenge people to be reconcilers for twelve God?**

After about twelve minutes, call the groups back together, and ask speakers from each group to briefly share some of the highlights of what they learned. Close this activity with these words, **"Jesus gives each of us who wear his name a chance to start over. He continues to call us to action, just as he has from the beginning. He is able to forgive us regardless of our sin. Finally, he renews his commission to us, entrusting us with the greatest challenge any have known. He calls us to be his disciples and to *make* disciples of all nations. In what areas of your lives do you need this fresh start?"**

Lecture Plus

Time: 20-25 minutes

Before class, prepare a brief lecture using the **Scripture Commentary**. Divide your lecture into three sections outlined below.

A. Jesus' call to us is unchanged over time.

Ask one or two volunteers to read John 21:1-14.

Distribute plain paper and colored pencils, crayons, or markers to all students. Ask them to draw a simple picture of one scene from this narrative. Say, **"You may

---

Materials Needed

↝ paper and colored pencils, crayons, or markers

use any perspective you want from the story. Draw your picture from the point of view of Jesus, Peter, John, or one of the other disciples. The goal is not to draw a great masterpiece, but to catch the essence of what is going on in this story." (Stick figures will work just fine!)

Give students about five minutes to draw their pictures. Then ask several volunteers to share their pictures and explain what is going on. Be sure to reward creativity and imagination!

Next, give a five to eight minute lecture using the **Scripture Commentary** from the beginning and through section 1, "Jesus' power is unchanged over time," as a reference.

Conclude by asking, **"How has God continued to call you into fellowship with him?"**

B. Jesus' forgiveness is always as great as our sin.

Before class, recruit three people to do a dramatic reading of John 21:15-17. The three volunteers will play the parts of Jesus, Peter, and the narrator. Encourage actors to speak their lines dramatically, using voice inflection and gestures. After the skit, thank actors for their participation.

Then give a five to eight minute lecture based on the **Scripture Commentary,** section 2, "Jesus' forgiveness is always as great as our sin."

Lead a brief discussion based on this question: **"Imagine you are Peter. What would be going through your mind during this conversation with Jesus?"** Ask, **"How did Jesus give Peter both a fresh start and a new focus?"**

C. Jesus' plan for us will continue to be challenging.

Ask a volunteer to read John 21:18-23.

Say, **"In verse 19, Jesus commanded Peter to 'Follow me!' This might remind you of the command Jesus gave Peter on a seashore about three years earlier, 'Come, follow me, and I will make you fishers of men' (Mark 1:17). With what did Jesus want Peter to be concerned?"**

Give a five to eight minute lecture based on the **Scripture Commentary,** section 3, "Jesus' plan for us will continue to be challenging."

Say, **"Imagine again that you are Peter. How would *you* react if Jesus told you that you would die in his service? Notice how Peter quickly asked about John. We can sometimes be more concerned with how other Christians are being called or rewarded than with what Jesus is calling us to do and be. Why do you think that is?"**

Close this activity with these words, **"Jesus gives each of us who wear his name a chance to start over. He continues to call us to action, just as he has from the beginning. He is able to forgive us regardless of our sin. Finally, he renews his commission to us, entrusting us with the greatest challenge any have known. He calls us to be his disciples and to *make* disciples of all nations. In what areas of your lives do you need this fresh start?"**

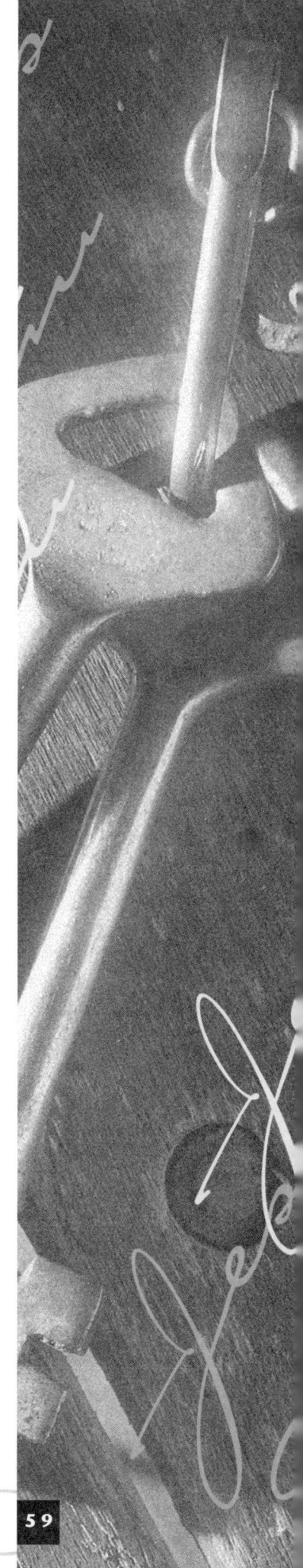

FREE INDEED

THE WORD BECAME FLESH...

Choose one of the options below to help students decide to make a fresh start in their relationships with God in a particular area of life.

Personal Paraphrase

Time: 15 minutes

Distribute copies of page 62 to each student. On it is printed 1 Peter 2:25. They are to consider the passage and paraphrase Peter's words as a confession that recalls the events of today's text. Format the paraphrase like this: **"I was _____, but now, _____."**

After doing so, have them personalize that paraphrase, using the same format. In this case, have them refer to events in their own lives.

After students have finished these tasks, allow volunteers to share their responses. Close this session by saying, **"Today is the day to make a fresh start with God. His name is 'I Am.' If you live in the past, God is not there. His name is not, 'I Was.' When you try to live in the future with its uncertainties, God is not there. His name is not 'I Will Be.' Today each of us can make a fresh start, regardless of what we have done. His name is 'I Am.'"**

The Follow-Through Factor

Time: 5 minutes

This section appears in every lesson in this series. This weekly devotion plan helps class members apply the Bible study throughout the coming week. You may use it immediately after the Bible study or in conjunction with the preceding activity.

Give each person a copy of the handout. Take time to briefly read through it, but do not discuss any of the questions at this time.

Close the session in prayer.

Materials Needed

- copies of page 62 for each student

Materials Needed

- one copy of "The Follow-Through Factor" handout from page 63 for each person

NOTES

LIFE IS AMAZING

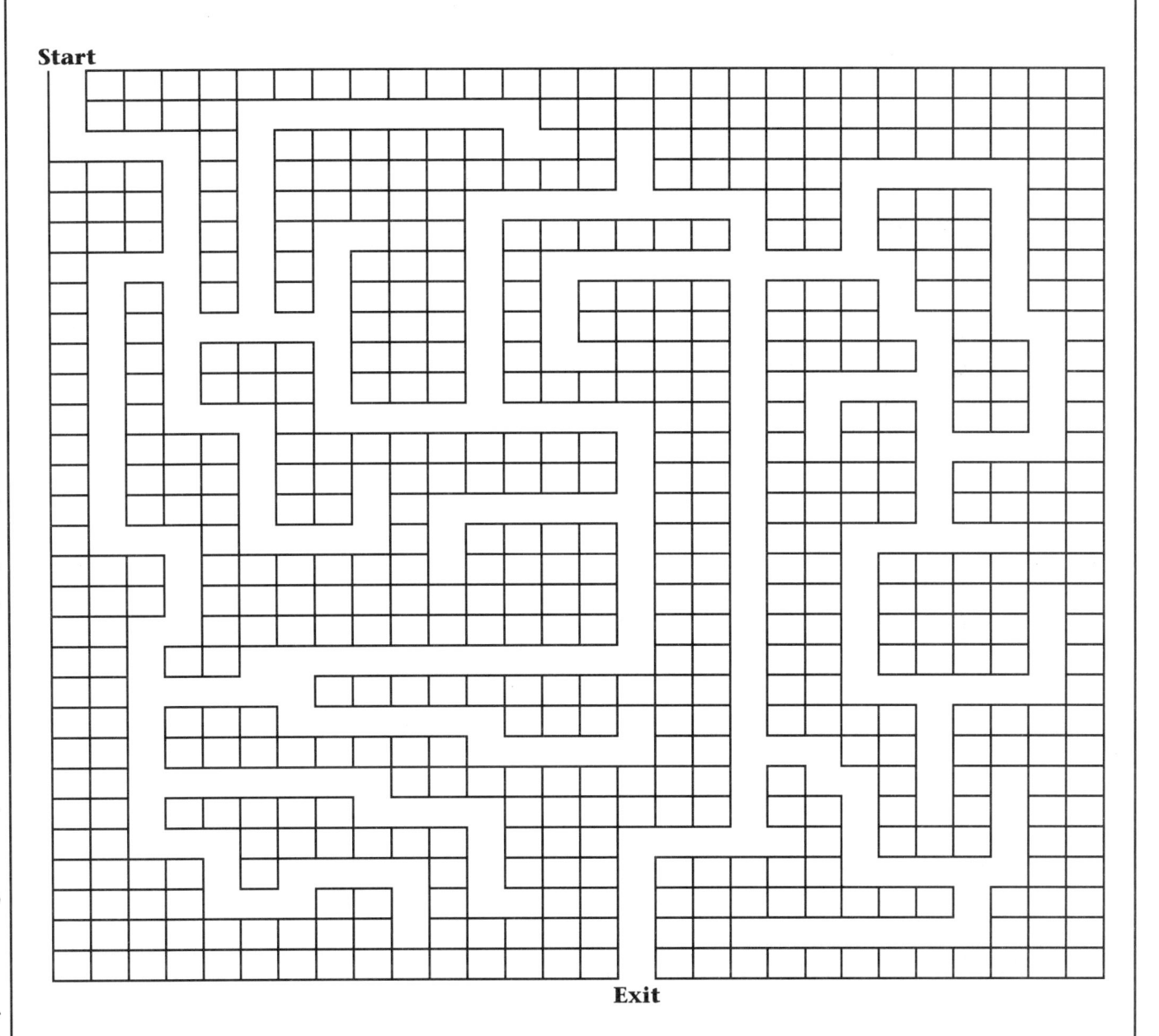

Start

Exit

PERSONAL PARAPHRASE

"For you were like sheep going astray, but now you have returned to the Shepherd and Overseer of your souls."
1 Peter 2:25

Consider the words of Peter above. Rewrite this passage as a confession of Peter that recalls the events of today's text.

I was _____
_____
_____
_____
_____
_____

But now _____
_____
_____
_____
_____
_____

Now personalize that paraphrase, using the same format. In this case, refer to events in your own life.

I was _____
_____
_____
_____
_____
_____

But now _____
_____
_____
_____
_____
_____

SOLID FOUNDATION BIBLE STUDIES

THE FOLLOW-THROUGH FACTOR
Jesus frees us from our past mistakes.

Consider the implications of your last Bible study through this next week.

Monday
Read Luke 5:5 and John 21:3-5.
In what areas of your life have you tried, without success, to work at on your own?
Take time to ask God for his intervention in this area.

Tuesday
Read John 21:7 and Matthew 14:28, 29.
When has been a time in your life when you "got out of your boat" to go to Jesus?
Prayerfully consider how you can "get out of your boat" today.

Wednesday
Read John 21:9-13 and Matthew 14:17-19.
How has God provided for your needs after a time of failing on your own?
Thank God for his provisions in your life and confess your dependence on him.

Thursday
Read John 21:16 and John 18:25.
If Jesus asked you, "Do you truly love me?" how would you respond? How does your life reflect that love? If you can truthfully do so, tell God that you love him and ask for his power to respond to him in a way that pleases him.

Friday
Read John 21:17-19 and Matthew 4:18-20.
What does it mean to you to follow Jesus? Prayerfully commit yourself to following Jesus today. Ask for his power and wisdom to follow him in your life.

Saturday
Read John 21:20-22 and Galatians 6:1-5
Consider a brother or sister in Christ of whom you are a bit envious. What have they experienced or not experienced that leads you to envy them? Rid yourself of that envy today.

LESSON 6

Coming in April 1999 from

SOLID FOUNDATION RESOURCES!

SOLID FOUNDATION BIBLE STUDIES

Wrestling With Life
Lessons from the Story of Jacob
by Bob Buller
Six sessions for adult classes from
Genesis 25–50

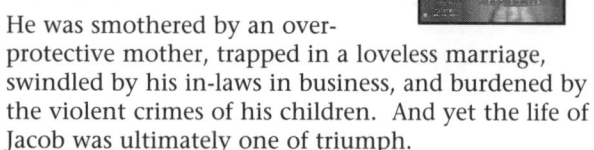

He was smothered by an overprotective mother, trapped in a loveless marriage, swindled by his in-laws in business, and burdened by the violent crimes of his children. And yet the life of Jacob was ultimately one of triumph.

Challenges to Faith
Lessons from the Early Church
by Paul Friskney
Six sessions for adult classes from
1 Corinthians

Men and women of faith have always struggled with difficult questions about life, the church, and God. The apostle Paul addressed the controversies in the church of Corinth with insight relevant to every age.

SOLID FOUNDATION SERMON STARTERS

God's Word is the foundation. Jesus is the cornerstone. Build on both with the sermon plans in these books!
Each outline is contained on the front and back of one perforated page for easy removal and use. Outlines include illustrations and examples to help provide a finishing touch to your presentation. Add to this framework for complete exegetical sermons customized for your congregation.

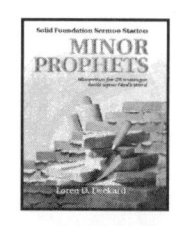

SOLID FOUNDATION MEDITATIONS

Create unique meditations for offering and Communion times!
Jesus often began instructing his followers by telling a story. After meeting his audience on the *common* ground of a familiar experience, he moved on with them to the *higher* ground of God's eternal truth.

The 52 meditations in each of these books are designed to follow that strategy. Each meditation uses Scripture and gives instructions for introducing it with a personal story. Includes helpful indexing and perforated pages.

Ask for them at your local Christian bookstore!